CAMBRIDGE
UNIVERSITY PRESS

Combined and Co-ordinated Sciences

for Cambridge IGCSE™

CHEMISTRY WORKBOOK

Joanna Haywood, Richard Harwood & Ian Lodge

CAMBRIDGE
UNIVERSITY PRESS

Shaftesbury Road, Cambridge CB2 8EA, United Kingdom

One Liberty Plaza, 20th Floor, New York, NY 10006, USA

477 Williamstown Road, Port Melbourne, VIC 3207, Australia

314–321, 3rd Floor, Plot 3, Splendor Forum, Jasola District Centre, New Delhi – 110025, India

103 Penang Road, #05–06/07, Visioncrest Commercial, Singapore 238467

Cambridge University Press is part of the University of Cambridge.

It furthers the University's mission by disseminating knowledge in the pursuit of education, learning and research at the highest international levels of excellence.

www.cambridge.org
Information on this title: www.cambridge.org/9781009311335

© Cambridge University Press & Assessment 2023

First published 2017
Second edition 2023

20 19 18 17 16 15 14 13 12 11 10 9 8 7 6 5 4

Printed in Poland by Opolgraf

A catalogue record for this publication is available from the British Library

ISBN 978-1-009-31133-5 Workbook with Digital Access

Additional resources for this publication at www.cambridge.org/9781009311335

Endorsement statement

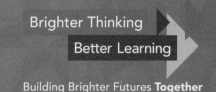

⟩ Contents

> How to use this series

We offer a comprehensive, flexible array of resources for the Combined and Co-ordinated Sciences syllabuses. We provide targeted support and practice for the specific challenges we've heard that students face: learning science with English as a second language; structured learning for all; and developing practical skills.

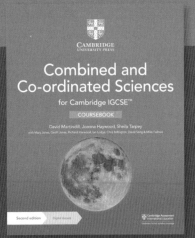

The coursebook provides coverage of the full Cambridge IGCSE™ Combined and Co-ordinated Sciences syllabuses. Each chapter explains facts and concepts, and uses relevant real-world examples of scientific principles to bring the subject to life. Together with a focus on practical work and plenty of active learning opportunities, the coursebook prepares learners for all aspects of their scientific study. Questions and practice questions in every chapter help learners to consolidate their understanding and provide practice opportunities to apply their learning.

The teacher's resource contains detailed guidance for all topics of the syllabuses, including common misconceptions identifying areas where learners might need extra support, as well as an engaging bank of lesson ideas for each syllabus topic. Differentiation is emphasised with advice for identification of different learner needs and suggestions of appropriate interventions to support and stretch learners. The teacher's resource also contains support for preparing and carrying out all the investigations in the practical workbook, including a set of sample results for when practicals aren't possible.

The teacher's resource also contains scaffolded worksheets and unit tests for each chapter. Answers for all components are accessible to teachers for free on the Cambridge GO platform.

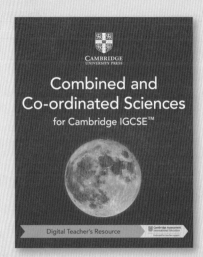

The skills-focused workbooks have been carefully constructed to help learners develop the skills that they need as they progress through their Cambridge IGCSE™ Combined and Co-ordinated Sciences course, providing further practice of some of the topics in the coursebook, each science with its own separate workbook. A three-tier, scaffolded approach to skills development enables students to gradually progress through 'focus', 'practice' and 'challenge' exercises, ensuring that every learner is supported. The workbooks enable independent learning and are ideal for use in class or as homework.

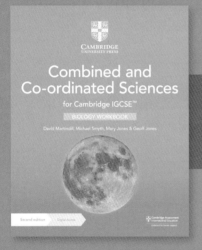

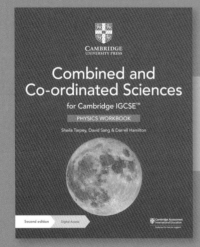

> How to use this book

Throughout this book, you will notice lots of different features that will help your learning. These are explained below.

LEARNING INTENTIONS

These set the scene for each exercise and indicate the important concepts.

KEY WORDS

Definitions for useful vocabulary are given at the start of each section. You will also find definitions for these words in the glossary at the back of this book.

KEY EQUATIONS

These boxes remind learners of important equations that are required to answer questions in a topic or exercise.

TIP

The information in these boxes will help you complete the exercises, and give you support in areas that you might find difficult.

Exercises

These help you to practise skills that are important for studying Cambridge IGCSE Chemistry.

Questions within exercises fall into one of three types:

- Focus questions will help build your basic skills.

- Practice questions provide more opportunities to test your knowledge, pushing your skills further.

- Challenge questions will stretch and challenge you even further.

SELF/PEER ASSESSMENT

At the end of some exercises, you will find opportunities to help you assess your own work, or that of your classmates, and consider how you can improve the way you learn.

> Introduction

This workbook covers two syllabuses: Cambridge IGCSE Combined Science (0653) and Cambridge IGCSE and IGCSE (9-1) Co-ordinated Sciences syllabuses (0654/0973). Before you start using this workbook, check with your teacher which syllabus you are studying and which papers you will take. You will sit either the Core paper or the Extended paper for your syllabus. If you are sitting the Extended paper, you will study the Core material and the Supplement material for your syllabus.

Once you know which paper you will be sitting, you can use the exercises in this workbook to help develop the skills you need and prepare for your examination.

The examination tests three different Assessment Objectives, or AOs for short. These are:

AO1 Knowledge with understanding

AO2 Handling information and problem solving

AO3 Experimental skills and investigations.

Just learning your work and remembering it is not enough to make sure that you achieve your best result in your exam. You also need to be able to use what you've learned in unfamiliar contexts (AO2) and to demonstrate your experimental skills (AO3).

There are lots of activities in your coursebook which will help you to develop your experimental skills by doing practical work. This workbook contains exercises to help you to develop AO2 and AO3 further. There are some questions that just involve remembering things you have been taught (AO1), but most of the questions require you to use what you've learned to work out, for example, what a set of data means, or to suggest how an experiment might be improved.

These exercises are not intended to be exactly like the questions you will get on your exam papers. This is because they are meant to help you to develop your skills, rather than testing you on them.

There's an introduction at the start of each exercise that tells you the purpose of it, and which skills you will be working with as you answer the questions.

There are sidebars in the margins of the book to show which material relates to each syllabus and paper. If there is no sidebar, it means that everyone will study this material.

Use this table to ensure that you study the right material for your syllabus and paper:

Cambridge IGCSE Combined Science (0653)		Cambridge IGCSE Co-ordinated Sciences (0654)	
Core	Supplement	Core	Supplement
You will study the material:	You will study the material:	You will study the material:	You will study **everything**, which includes the material:
Without a sidebar	Without a sidebar	Without a sidebar	Without a sidebar
	With a dashed grey sidebar	With a solid grey sidebar	With a dashed grey sidebar
	With a dashed black sidebar	With a dashed black sidebar	With a dashed black sidebar
	You will <u>not</u> study material with a solid grey sidebar or a solid black sidebar.	You will <u>not</u> study material with a solid black sidebar or a dashed grey sidebar.	With a solid grey sidebar
			With a solid black sidebar

A simplified table has also been included on the inside back flap of this workbook to open out and view alongside the exercises.

Safety

A few practical exercises have been included. These could be carried out at home using simple materials that you are likely to have available to you.

While carrying out such experiments, it is your responsibility to think about your own safety, and the safety of others. Work sensibly, under supervision, and assess any risks before starting. If you are in doubt, discuss what you are going to do with your teacher before you start.

Chapter 1
States of matter

> Solids, liquids and gases

Exercise 1.1

KEY WORDS

boiling: the process of change from liquid to gas at the boiling point of the substance; a condition under which gas bubbles are able to form within a liquid – gas molecules escape from the body of the liquid, not just from its surface.

evaporation: a process occurring at the surface of a liquid, involving the change of state from a liquid into a vapour at a temperature below the boiling point.

freezing point: the temperature at which a liquid turns into solid – it has the same value as the melting point; a pure substance has a sharp freezing point.

Focus

1   There are three states of matter, which have different basic physical properties. Complete the sentences by adding two properties shown by each physical state.

A solid has a fixed _____ and _____.

A liquid has a fixed _____ but its _____ changes to match that of the container in which it is placed.

A gas has no fixed _____ or _____. A gas completely fills the container it is in.

2   Complete the boxes below to show how the particles of a substance are arranged in the three states of matter.

solid   liquid   gas

Practice

Question 2 showed the differences in structure and organisation of the particles between the three states. The differences can also be expressed in words. Table 1.1 describes the arrangement of the particles in four different substances: A, B, C and D.

Substance	Distance between particles	Arrangement of particles	Movement of particles
A	very far apart	randomly arranged	moving about with high speed
B	very close together	regularly ordered	vibrating about fixed positions
C	very far apart	regularly ordered	vibrating about fixed positions
D	close together	irregularly arranged	moving about

Table 1.1: The arrangement and movement of particles in substances A, B, C and D.

3 Which of substances A, B, C and D is:

    a   a solid   ....

    b   unlikely to be a real substance   ....

    c   a gas   ....

    d   a liquid?   ....

4 Changing the temperature can cause a substance to change its physical state. What are the changes of state labelled A, B, C and D in Figure 1.1?

    (*Note:* sublimation is not required knowledge.)

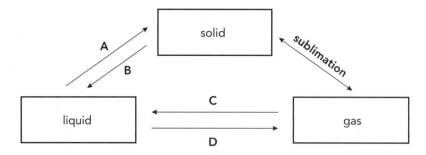

Figure 1.1: Changes of physical state.

A ....   B ....

C ....   D ....

Challenge

5   Table 1.2 provides data about the melting and boiling points of different
substances at atmospheric pressure. Use these data to answer the questions.

Substance	Melting point/°C	Boiling point/°C
sodium	98	883
radon	−71	−62
ethanol	−117	78
cobalt	1492	2900
nitrogen	−210	−196
propane	−188	−42
ethanoic acid	16	118

Table 1.2: Melting points and boiling points of various substances at
atmospheric pressure.

a   Which substance is a liquid over the smallest range of temperatures?

....

b   Which two substances are gaseous at −50 °C?

....

c   Which substance has the lowest freezing point?

....

d   Which substance is liquid at 2500 °C?

....

e   A sample of ethanoic acid was found to boil at 121 °C at
atmospheric pressure. Use the information in Table 1.2 to comment
on this result.

....

....

> **TIP**
>
> Be careful when
> dealing with
> temperatures below
> 0 °C. Remember
> that −100 °C is a
> higher temperature
> than −150 °C.

Exercise 1.2

IN THIS EXERCISE YOU WILL:

- develop your understanding of the changes in organisation and movement of particles that take place as a substance changes state

- use data from an experiment to plot a cooling curve for a substance

- link the different changes of state to the kinetic particle theory of matter and explain the changes taking place.

Focus

A student carried out a data-logging experiment as part of a project on changes of state. An organic crystalline solid was placed in a tube in a boiling water-bath, as shown in Figure 1.2. When the solid had melted, a temperature sensor was placed in the liquid.

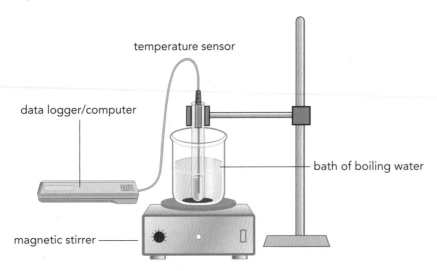

Figure 1.2: Using a temperature sensor to plot a cooling curve.

The data logger recorded the temperature of the liquid as it cooled to room temperature. Some of the data is shown in Table 1.3.

Time / minutes	0	0.5	1.0	1.5	2.0	2.2	2.4	2.6	2.8	3.0	3.5	4.0	4.5	5.0
Temperature / °C	96.1	89.2	85.2	82.0	80.9	80.7	80.6	80.6	80.5	80.3	78.4	74.2	64.6	47.0

Table 1.3: Results for a cooling curve experiment.

1 On the grid provided, plot a graph of the temperature change that took place in this experiment.

2 The student decided to repeat the experiment using a compound with a melting point greater than 100 °C. What change would she need to make to carry out the experiment?

....

3 What change is taking place between minutes 2 and 3 of the experiment?

....

Practice

4 Why does the temperature remain almost constant during the third minute of the experiment? When giving your answer, think about changes to the organisation of the molecules in the substance.

....

....

....

....

....

....

> **TIP**
>
> Pure substances have definite, precise melting points and boiling points. When a substance contains impurities, the melting and boiling points change and become less precise (spread over a range of temperatures).

5 Another student carried out a similar experiment to demonstrate the cooling curve for paraffin wax.

a In the space provided, sketch the shape of the graph you would expect the student to produce.

b Explain why you chose this shape for the curve you drew in part **a**.

....

....

Challenge

6   Cooling curve experiments can be reversed, allowing students to plot a heating curve instead. Figure 1.3 shows the heating curve for a pure substance. The temperature rises over time as the substance is heated.

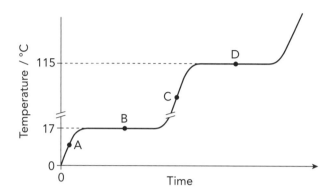

Figure 1.3: A heating curve for a pure substance.

a   In what physical state(s) is the substance at points A, B, C and D?

   A   ....

   B   ....

   C   ....

   D   ....

b   What is the melting point of the substance?

   ....

c   What is the boiling point of the substance?

   ....

d   How does the temperature change while the substance is changing state?

   ....

e   The substance is not water. How do you know this from the graph?

   ....

7 The solid form of carbon dioxide is known as dry ice. Dry ice is used in commercial refrigeration and to create spectacular and misty stage effects. The surface of dry ice at atmospheric pressure is different from the surface of ordinary water ice: there is no liquid film on it.

   a If you gently shake a fire extinguisher filled with carbon dioxide (Figure 1.4), you will feel the presence of liquid within the extinguisher. What conditions within the extinguisher allow the carbon dioxide to exist as a liquid?

   ....

   ....

Figure 1.4: A carbon dioxide fire extinguisher.

   b Frost is ice crystals that form on surfaces when conditions are very cold. Using the words provided, complete the following paragraph about a particular type of frost known as hoar frost.

   colder   crystals   humid   ice

   liquid   surrounding   white

   Hoar frost is a powdery _____ frost caused when solid _____

   forms from _____ air.

   The solid surface on which it is formed must be _____ than the

   _____ air.

   Water vapour is deposited on a surface as fine ice _____ without

   going through the _____ phase.

c For most substances, the change from a solid to a gas involves a liquid phase.
The change from liquid to gas takes place by evaporation and/or boiling.
Use the ideas of kinetic particle theory to explain the difference between
these two processes.

evaporation: ....

....

....

....

....

....

boiling: ....

....

....

....

....

....

SELF ASSESSMENT

Use this checklist to give yourself a mark for the graph you drew in question 1.
For each point, award yourself:

2 marks   if you did it really well

1 mark   if you made a good attempt and partly succeeded

0 marks   if you did not try to do it, or did not succeed.

Then ask your teacher to mark you on the skills as well.

Checklist	Marks awarded	
	You	Your teacher
Have you drawn the axes with a ruler, using most of the width and height of the grid?		
Have you used a sensible scale for the x-axis and the y-axis, which goes up in easily managed units (1 minute, 2 minutes, etc.)? (*Note:* the axes do not necessarily need to start at the origin $(0,0)$.)		
Have you labelled the axes correctly? Have you given the correct units for the scales on both axes?		
Have you plotted each point precisely and correctly?		
Have you used a small neat cross or encircled dot for each point?		
Have you drawn a single, clear best-fit line through each set of points?		
Have you ignored any anomalous (unexpected) results when drawing the line through each set of points?		
Total (out of 14):		

Your total score will reflect how clear and well-presented your graph is. You should be able to deduce reliable information from your graph.

Look at the scores in the table. What did you do well? What aspects will you focus on next time?
Talk with your teacher and ask for advice to help you improve your presentation of graphical data.

〉 Diffusion

Exercise 1.3

IN THIS EXERCISE YOU WILL:

- consider how the process of diffusion explains how a solid can dissolve in a liquid

- examine how diffusion in a liquid or gas results from the spreading of particles to fill the space available to them

- consider the relationship between the rate of diffusion in gases and their molecular mass.

KEY WORD

diffusion: the process by which different fluids mix as a result of the random motions of their particles.

Focus

1   A student placed some crystals of potassium manganate(VII) at the bottom of a beaker of distilled water. She left the contents of the beaker to stand for one hour. Figure 1.5 shows what she saw during the experiment. After one hour, the student observed that all the solid crystals had disappeared and the solution was purple throughout.

distilled water

purple crystals

at start   after 15 minutes   after 1 hour

Figure 1.5: Crystals of potassium manganate(VII) placed in water.

a   Use the ideas of diffusion to explain the student's observations.

You may wish to use some or all of these phrases in your answer.

crystal surface	**evenly spread**	**particles move**
solid dissolves completely	**spread out**	**the crystals are soluble**

....

....

....

....

b If the student had used warm water at 50 °C, would the observations have taken place in a longer or shorter time? Explain your answer.

....

....

....

Practice

2 Ammonium chloride is an example of a compound that can change from a solid to a gas, without passing through a liquid stage (Figure 1.6). The white solid changes directly to the vapour state when it is heated. The solid then reforms on the cooler upper part of the tube.

Figure 1.6: Heating ammonium chloride.

In fact, these changes in state of ammonium chloride involve two chemical reactions. The first reaction is the thermal decomposition of the solid ammonium chloride. The products are two gases: ammonia and hydrogen chloride.

a Write a word equation for the decomposition of ammonium chloride.

....

b In the cooler part of the tube the two gases react to form ammonium chloride. Complete the following chemical equation for this reaction. Include the state symbol for the missing reactant.

$NH_3(g) +$ .... $\rightarrow NH_4Cl(s)$

Challenge

3 Figure 1.7 shows a laboratory demonstration of the reaction between ammonia and hydrogen chloride. The apparatus is arranged so that the two gases, ammonia and hydrogen chloride, diffuse towards each other in a sealed tube.

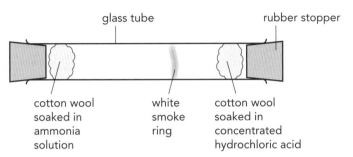

Figure 1.7: Demonstration of the different rates of diffusion for gases.

Where the gases meet within the sealed tube, they react to form a white smoke ring of ammonium chloride.

a The white solid forms nearer the end of the tube containing the concentrated hydrochloric acid. Explain why.

....

....

....

b The distance between the cotton wool balls is 45 cm. Approximately how far from the end of the tube containing the ammonia will the white ring form?

....

....

Table 1.4 shows the formulae and relative molecular masses of four different gases.

Gas	Formula	Relative molecular mass (M_r)
oxygen	O_2	32
hydrogen	H_2	2
chlorine	Cl_2	71
methane	CH_4	16

Table 1.4: Formulae and relative molecular masses of several gases.

c List the four gases in order of their rate of diffusion (with the quickest first).

....

....

d A gas, G, diffuses more slowly than methane but more quickly than oxygen. What can you say about the relative molecular mass of G?

....

....

> **TIP**
>
> When you are asked to list things in increasing or decreasing order, make sure you use the 'greater than' (>) and 'less than' (<) symbols correctly.

4 Complete these paragraphs using the words provided.

> **different   diffuse   diffusion   gas   lattice molecular**
>
> **inversely   particles   random   spread   temperature   vibrate**

The kinetic model states that the _____ in a liquid and in a _____ are constantly moving. In a gas, the particles are far apart from each other and their movement is said to be _____. The particles in a solid are held in fixed positions in a regular _____. In a solid, the particles can only _____ about their fixed positions.

Liquids and gases are fluids. When particles move in a fluid, they can collide with each other. When they collide, they bounce off each other in _____ directions. If two gases or liquids are mixed, the different types of particle _____ out and get mixed up. This process is called _____.

In gases at the same _____, particles that have a lower mass move more quickly than particles with higher mass. This means that the lighter particles spread and mix more quickly. The lighter particles are said to _____ more quickly than the heavier particles. When gaseous molecules diffuse, the rate at which they do so is _____ related to the relative _____ mass (M_r) of the gas.

> Chapter 2
Atoms, elements and compounds

> Elements, compounds and mixtures

Exercise 2.1

IN THIS EXERCISE YOU WILL:
• review the key differences between elements, compounds and mixtures
• understand the representation of these different substances in diagrams.

KEY WORD

compound: a substance formed by the chemical combination of two or more elements in fixed proportions.

Focus

1 Using the words provided, complete the table to show the differences between a compound and a mixture. Some words may be used more than once.

any   combined   definite   different

elements   physical   present   properties   separated

Compound	Mixture
The _____ cannot be _____ by _____ methods.	The substances in it can be _____ by _____ methods.
The properties of a compound are _____ from those of the _____ that make it.	The substances _____ still show the same _____ as they have by themselves.
The elements are _____ in a _____ proportion by mass.	The substances can be _____ in _____ proportions by mass.

Table 2.1: Comparison of compounds and mixtures.

Practice

2   Look at this list of everyday substances. Some of them are chemical compounds and others are mixtures.

air   brass   carbon dioxide   copper sulfate

distilled water   hydrochloric acid solution   lemonade

seawater   sodium chloride

Which of these substances are:

a   compounds?

....

....

b   mixtures?

....

....

KEY WORDS

element: a substance which cannot be further divided into simpler substances by chemical methods; all the atoms of an element contain the same number of protons.

mixture: two or more substances mixed together but not chemically combined; the substances can be separated by physical means.

3   Figure 2.1 shows six different substances. Each circle represents an atom.
    State whether each substance is a pure element, a pure compound or a mixture.

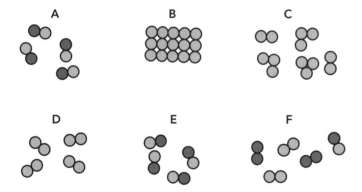

Figure 2.1: Arrangement of atoms in six different structures.

A   ....   B   ....

C   ....   D   ....

E   ....   F   ....

Challenge

4   The following paragraph describes the reaction between sodium and chlorine.

Sodium is a silvery-grey metal that reacts violently with water. Chlorine is a green gas which is toxic and dissolves in water to give a weakly acidic solution. When sodium reacts with chlorine, heat is given out and a white powder (sodium chloride) is formed. Sodium chloride dissolves in water to give a neutral solution.

What information in this paragraph tells us that sodium chloride is a compound and not a mixture?

....

....

....

....

5   Iron is a grey magnetic metal that reacts with hydrochloric acid to produce hydrogen gas. Sulfur is a yellow non-metal that does not react with acids.

Powders of these two elements can be mixed and heated together in a test-tube. The mixture glows red on heating and continues to glow red even when the tube is removed from the Bunsen burner flame.

After heating the mixture, a black powder is produced. This powder is not magnetic and reacts with hydrochloric acid to give a smelly gas, hydrogen sulfide.

Use these observations to answer the following questions.

a   State *three* differences between the two elements, iron and sulfur.

....

....

....

b   Explain why it is important that the mixture continues to glow with heat after it is removed from the flame.

....

....

c   Give *two* pieces of evidence that a compound is formed when the powders are heated together.

....

....

› Atomic structure and the Periodic Table, and isotopes

Exercise 2.2

IN THIS EXERCISE YOU WILL:

- see how the structure of any atom is defined by its proton (atomic) number and mass (nucleon) number

- learn how the electrons in an atom are organised in shells around the nucleus

- find out how the electronic configuration of an atom relates to its position in the Periodic Table of elements.

Focus

Dalton's atomic theory suggested that atoms were indivisible particles, from which all elements were made. We have since found that atoms are made up of smaller subatomic particles. Each element is made up of atoms with different – and characteristic – numbers of subatomic particles.

1   Complete the text using the words provided. Words may be used once, more than once or not at all.

electrons   nucleon   nucleus   proton

protons   shells

Atoms are made up of three different particles:

- _____, which are positively charged

- _____, which have no charge

- _____, which are negatively charged.

The negatively charged particles are arranged in different _____ (energy levels) around the _____ of the atom. These particles, _____, have a negligible mass. All atoms of the same element contain the same number of _____ and _____.

KEY WORDS

electron: a subatomic particle with negligible mass and a charge of −1; electrons are present in all atoms, located in shells (energy levels) outside the nucleus.

electronic configuration: a shorthand method of describing the arrangement of electrons within the electron shells (or energy levels) of an atom; also referred to as electronic structure.

electron shells (energy levels): (of electrons) the allowed energies of electrons in atoms; electrons fill these shells (or levels) starting with the one closest to the nucleus.

isotopes: atoms of the same element which have the same proton number but a different nucleon number; they have different numbers of neutrons in their nuclei; some isotopes are radioactive because their nuclei are unstable (radioisotopes).

neutron: an uncharged subatomic particle present in the nuclei of atoms; a neutron has a mass of 1 relative to a proton.

2   An atom of lithium has three protons and a nucleon number of 7.

    a   How many electrons are in the lithium atom? ....

    b   How many neutrons does lithium have? ....

    c   What is the mass number of this lithium atom? ....

    d   Describe the lithium atom in the format that uses two numbers and the symbol for the element.

    ....

Practice

3   This part of the exercise is concerned with electronic configurations and the structure of the Periodic Table. Complete the text by filling in the missing words or numbers.

The electrons in an atom are arranged in a series of _____ around the

central nucleus. These shells are also called _____ levels. In an atom,

the shell _____ to the nucleus fills first, then the next shell, and so on.

There is room for:

- up to _____ electrons in the first shell

- up to _____ electrons in the second shell

- up to _____ electrons in the third shell.

(For elements up to calcium, Z = 20, there are 18 electrons in total when the three shells are full.)

The elements in the Periodic Table are organised in the same way as the

electrons fill the shells. Shells fill from _____ to _____ across the

_____ of the Periodic Table.

- The first shell fills up first, from _____ to helium.

- The second shell fills next, from lithium to _____.

- Eight _____ go into the third shell, from sodium to argon.

- Then the fourth shell starts to fill, from potassium.

KEY WORDS

nucleon: a particle present in the nucleus of an atom.

proton: a subatomic particle with a relative atomic mass of 1 and a charge of +1, found in the nucleus of all atoms.

subatomic particles: very small particles – protons, neutrons and electrons – from which all atoms are made (*Note:* the term subatomic particles is useful but you do not need to learn it).

TIP

You can show the electronic configuration of an atom by writing the numbers of electrons in a list, starting from the first shell (for example, 2,8,4 for silicon). Alternatively, you can draw the structure as a diagram, with electrons shown orbiting the nucleus of the atom. At IGCSE, you are only expected to be able to give the electronic configurations of the first 20 elements in the Periodic Table.

Challenge

4 Use the Periodic Table to help you name the following elements.

a the element with 2 electrons in the first shell, 8 in the second and 2 in the third

....

b the element with 2 electrons in the first shell and 7 in the second

....

c the element with 2 electrons in the first shell, 8 in the second, 8 in the third and 1 in the fourth.

....

5 Give the names of the following:

a the element in Group III, Period 2

....

b the element in Group V, Period 3.

....

6 Complete the electronic arrangement of the Group II elements in Table 2.2.

	First shell	Second shell	Third shell	Fourth shell
Beryllium	2	2	–	–
Magnesium		8		–
Calcium	2	8		

Table 2.2: The electronic arrangements of some Group II elements.

> **TIP**
>
> Use the Periodic Table at the back of this workbook to help you work out the composition of subatomic particles in any atom. For example, magnesium is the 12th atom in the Periodic Table, so it must have 12 protons and 12 electrons in its atoms.

SELF ASSESSMENT

Which parts of this exercise did you find easy? Which parts were difficult? Put a tick (✓) or cross (✗) next to each statement:

• I feel confident defining a proton, a neutron and an electron. ☐

• I feel confident describing the atomic structure of the first 20 elements of the Periodic Table. ☐

• I can clearly describe the relationship between atomic structure and the Periodic Table. ☐

Exercise 2.3

Focus

1   Table 2.3 gives details of the atomic structure of five atoms: A, B, C, D and E.

   a   Complete the table to show the electronic configuration of each atom.

Atom	Proton number	Electronic configuration			
		1st shell	2nd shell	3rd shell	4th shell
A	2				
B	5				
C	13				
D	15				
E	19				

Table 2.3: Table of electronic configurations.

   b   How many of these atoms are of elements in the second period of the Periodic Table?

   ....

   c   Which *two* atoms belong to elements in the same group?

   ....

d How many electrons does atom C have which would be involved in chemical bonding?

....

e Figure 2.2 shows the arrangement of electrons in the shells (energy levels) of atom B. Using this as a guide, draw a diagram in the space provided to show the arrangement of the electrons in Atom D.

Atom B   **Atom D**

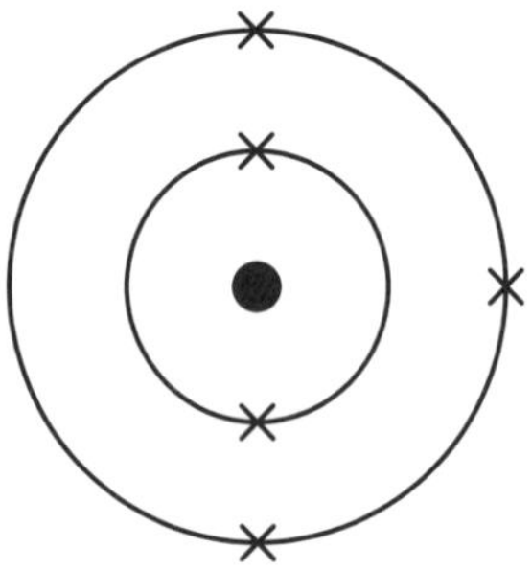

Figure 2.2: The electron arrangements of atoms B and D.

Practice

2 In 1986, an explosion at Chernobyl in Ukraine released a radioactive cloud containing various radioactive isotopes. Three of these isotopes are given in Table 2.4. Use the Periodic Table found at the back of the book to answer the following questions about them.

Element	Mass (nucleon) number
strontium	90
iodine	131
caesium	137

Table 2.4: Isotopes released at Chernobyl.

> **TIP**
>
> Any atom is electrically neutral. The two defining numbers for any atom – the proton (atomic) number and the mass (nucleon) number – can be used to work out the composition of subatomic particles.

a How many electrons are in one atom of strontium-90? ....

b How many protons are in one atom of iodine-131? ....

c How many neutrons are in one atom of iodine-131? ....

d How many neutrons are in one atom of caesium-137? ....

e Define *isotope*.

....

....

3   Figure 2.3 shows the structures of five atoms: A, B, C, D and E.

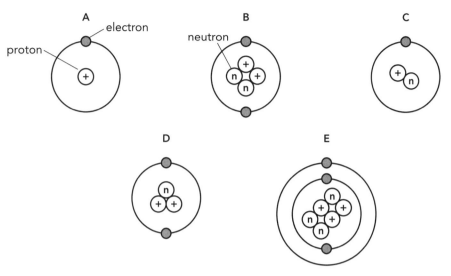

Figure 2.3: Atomic structure of five atoms, A–E.

Answer the following questions about the atoms. Each structure may be used once, more than once, or not at all.

a   Which structure has a mass number of 4? ....

b   Which structure represents the atom of a metal? ....

c   Which two atoms are isotopes of each other? ....

d   Which structures are isotopes of helium? ....

Challenge

The characteristic properties of an atom are related to the organisation of the subatomic particles within that atom. This organisation determines important properties of the atom, such as: whether it is radioactive; the type of bonds it makes; its chemical reactivity; and its position in the Periodic Table.

4   The modern view of the structure of the atom comes from experiments using α-particles (helium nuclei). These particles were fired at a sheet of gold foil from a radioactive source. Detectors analysed the direction of the particles as they passed through the foil. The design of the experiment is summarised in Figure 2.4.

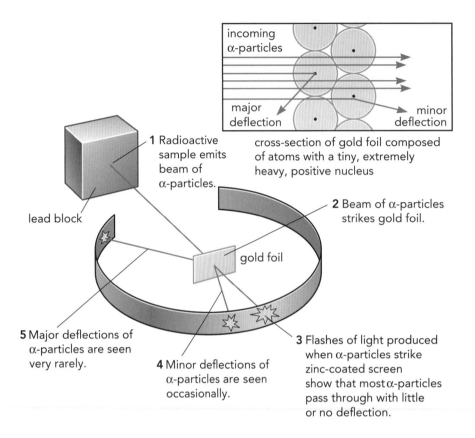

Figure 2.4: The Geiger and Marsden experiment. (*Note:* this experiment is not required knowledge.)

a α-particles are helium nuclei. What is the composition of an α-particle and its charge?

protons: ....

neutrons: ....

charge: ....

b Gold foil is a solid metal. How are the atoms of gold arranged in the foil? (*Note:* you may need to do some research to answer this question.)

....

....

c Most of the α-particles passed straight through the foil. What does this suggest about the structure of the atoms?

....

....

d Remarkably, some α-particles were repelled back in the direction from which they came. What part of the structure of the atom did these particles hit? Why were the particles repelled backwards?

....

....

5 The isotopes of some elements, such as carbon-14, are used in biochemical and medical research. These isotopes are radioactive, so scientists can use them to track the synthesis and use of important compounds in the chemistry of cells and tissues.

a Complete Table 2.5 about the isotopes of some common elements. You will need to make deductions from the information given. For each element, the second isotope is a radioisotope used in research.

Isotope	Name of element	Atomic number	Mass (nucleon) number	Number of		
				protons	neutrons	electrons
$^{12}_{6}C$	carbon	6	12	6	6	6
$^{14}_{6}C$						
$^{1}_{1}H$			1			
$^{3}_{1}H$	hydrogen (tritium)					
$^{31}_{15}P$		15	31			
$^{32}_{15}P$						
$^{127}_{53}I$	iodine			53		53
$^{131}_{53}I$				53		

Table 2.5: The isotopes of certain elements.

b Researchers can use these radioisotopes to study the chemistry of cells because these atoms have the same chemical properties as the non-radioactive atoms. Why are the chemical properties of all isotopes of the same element identical?

....

....

....

....

....

....

> Chemical bonding, ions and ionic bonds, and simple molecules and covalent bonds

Exercise 2.4

KEY WORDS

covalent bonding: chemical bonding formed by the sharing of one or more pairs of electrons between two atoms.

displayed formula: a representation of the structure of a compound which shows all the atoms and bonds in the molecule.

giant ionic lattice (structure): a lattice held together by the electrostatic forces of attraction between positive and negative ions.

IN THIS EXERCISE YOU WILL:

- describe the nature of ionic bonding and the properties of ionic compounds

- use the nature of the type of bond formed to explain some of the physical properties of the substances involved.

Focus

1   Figure 2.5 shows a model of the structure of sodium chloride and similar ionic crystals. The ions are arranged in a regular lattice structure of alternating positive and negative ions. This is known as a giant ionic lattice.

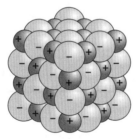

Figure 2.5: A giant ionic lattice.

a   How does the electronic configuration of a sodium cation differ from that of a sodium atom?

....

b   How does the electronic configuration of a chloride anion differ from that of a chlorine atom?

....

c Draw a dot-and-cross diagram to show the ions in sodium chloride.

TIP

Ionic compounds do not conduct electricity when solid. This is because the ions present are not free to move – they can only vibrate about fixed points in the structure.

d What type of forces of attraction hold the structure of sodium chloride together?

....

e Why does sodium chloride have a high melting point?

....

....

Practice

2 The boxes contain properties of ionic compounds and explanations of these properties. Draw lines to link each property box with the correct explanation.

Property	Explanation
A solution of an ionic compound in water is a good conductor of electricity. These ionic substances are called electrolytes.	The ions in the giant ionic structure always have the same regular arrangement.
Ionic crystals have a regular shape. The crystals of each solid ionic compound are the same shape. The angles between the faces of the crystal are always the same, whatever the size of the crystal.	Strong attraction between the positive and negative ions holds the giant ionic structure together. A lot of energy is needed to break down the regular arrangement of ions.
Ionic compounds have relatively high melting points.	In a molten ionic compound, the positive and negative ions can move. The ions can move to the electrodes when a voltage is applied.
A molten ionic compound (i.e. an ionic compound heated above its melting point) is a good conductor of electricity.	In a solution of an ionic compound, the positive metal ions and the negative non-metal ions can move. These ions can move to the electrodes when a voltage is applied.

Challenge

3 Dot-and-cross diagrams are used to show the movement of electrons in the formation of ionic bonds.

a Use dot-and-cross diagrams to represent the formation of magnesium oxide from magnesium atoms and oxygen molecules.

b Describe, in terms of movement of electrons and subsequent charges formed, how magnesium oxide is formed.

....

....

....

....

....

....

Exercise 2.5

IN THIS EXERCISE YOU WILL:

- describe how to draw the structures of simple covalent molecules

- draw dot-and-cross diagrams of the bonding in covalent molecules.

TIP

When drawing the displayed formula of a molecule it is important to show all the bonds. Make it clear whether they are single, double or even triple bonds.

Focus

1   Many covalent compounds exist as simple molecules, with the atoms joined together by single or double bonds. A covalent bond, made up of a shared pair of electrons, is often represented by a short straight line. Complete Table 2.6 by filling in the blank spaces.

Name of compound	Formula	Displayed formula	Molecular model
hydrogen chloride		H—Cl	
water	H_2O		
ammonia			
	CH_4		
ethene			
		O=C=O	

Table 2.6: The structure of some simple covalent molecules.

Practice

2   Complete Table 2.7 by drawing dot-and-cross diagrams and displayed formulae to represent the bonding in the following simple molecular compounds. In the dot-and-cross diagrams, show only the outer shells of the atoms involved.

Molecule	Dot-and-cross diagram	Displayed formula
ammonia (NH_3)		
water (H_2O)		
hydrogen chloride (HCl)		

Table 2.7: Diagrams representing the covalent bonding in different simple molecules.

Challenge

3   Complete Table 2.8 by drawing dot-and-cross and displayed formulae to represent
    the bonding in the following more complex molecular elements and compounds.
    Some of the diagrams involve multiple bonding.

Molecule	Dot-and-cross diagram	Displayed formula
nitrogen (N_2)		
ethene (C_2H_4)		
methanol (CH_3OH)		

Table 2.8: The covalent bonding in some elements and compounds.

PEER ASSESSMENT

Share your drawings with a partner and check that they can understand what you have drawn.
Ask them to use the following checklist:

☐ A correct dot-and-cross diagram and displayed formula have been drawn for each of the
  molecular compounds.

☐ The dot-and-cross diagrams clearly show the bonding in a molecule.

☐ Only the outer electrons have been included.

Discuss the checklist with your partner. Is there anything you could improve upon next time you draw
these diagrams?

> Giant covalent structures and metallic bonding

Exercise 2.6

KEY WORDS

giant covalent structure: a substance where large numbers of atoms are held together by covalent bonds forming a strong lattice structure.

IN THIS EXERCISE YOU WILL:

- describe the covalent structures of diamond and graphite
- relate the structures of diamond and graphite to their physical properties
- consider the bonding in a metal and relate this to metal properties.

Focus

1   This question considers some of the macromolecular forms of carbon.

   a   Complete this sentence.

   There are several different forms of carbon. Two of them are called

   _____ and _____ .

   b   Complete Table 2.9 to describe the arrangement of the atoms and the bonding present in diamond and graphite.

	Diamond	Graphite
Diagram		
Type of bonding		
Number of bonds formed by each carbon atom		
Geometry around each carbon atom		

Table 2.9: Structure and bonding in diamond and graphite.

c   Table 2.10 contains observations and explanations for the structures of diamond and graphite. Complete the table by filling in the gaps. The first section of the table has been completed for you; other sections are only partly complete.

Observation	Explanation
Diamond is a very hard substance …	… because all the atoms in the structure are joined by strong covalent bonds.
Diamond does not conduct electricity …	… because _____ _____
Graphite is _____ …	… because the layers in the structure are only held together by weak forces.
_____	… because there are some free electrons that are able to move between the layers to carry the current.

Table 2.10: The properties of diamond and graphite.

Practice

2   Graphite is one of the crystalline forms of carbon. Two of the distinctive properties of graphite are:

*   it conducts electricity even though it is a non-metal
*   it can act as a lubricant even though it has a giant covalent structure.

Give a brief explanation of these properties, considering the structure of graphite.

a   Graphite as an electrical conductor

....

....

....

b   Graphite as a lubricant

....

....

....

Challenge

3 **a** Complete Figure 2.6 to show the nature of metallic bonding, by adding in any other particles that are required and labelling the diagram.

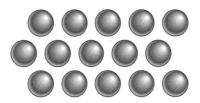

Figure 2.6: Metallic bonding.

b Use the information from your diagram to explain the following properties of metals.

i Many metals have a high melting temperature.

....

....

ii Metals are ductile.

....

....

iii All metals conduct electricity.

....

....

› Chapter 3
Stoichiometry

› Chemical formulae and equations

Exercise 3.1

IN THIS EXERCISE YOU WILL:

• construct the formulae of ionic and covalent compounds.

Focus

1 How many atoms of the different elements are there in the formulae of the following compounds?

    a nitric acid, HNO_3 ....

    b copper(II) nitrate, $Cu(NO_3)_2$ ....

    c ammonium sulfate, $(NH_4)_2SO_4$ ....

    d potassium manganate(VII), $KMnO_4$ ....

2 **a** Complete Figure 3.1 by adding the valencies (combining power) of the atoms shown.

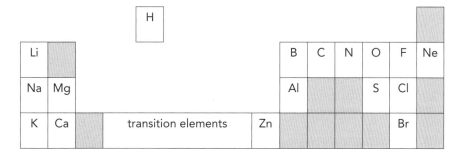

Figure 3.1: A section of the Periodic Table.

    b Which atoms in Figure 3.1 lose electrons when they form ions?

    ....

    c Which atoms in Figure 3.1 gain electrons when they form ions?

    ....

KEY WORDS

balanced chemical (symbol) equation: a summary of a chemical reaction using chemical formulae; the total number of any of the atoms involved is the same on both the reactant and product sides of the equation.

compound ion: an ion made up of several different atoms covalently bonded together and with an overall charge (can also be called a molecular ion; negatively charged compound ions containing oxygen can be called oxyanions).

ionic equation: a simplified equation for a reaction involving ionic substances; only the ions which actually take part in the reaction are shown.

d Name *two* atoms in Figure 3.1 that share electrons when they form compounds.

....

3 Write the formulae of the following compounds by balancing (or crossing over) the valencies. Use the position of each element in the Periodic Table to help you remember its valency.

a a compound of H and S ....

b a compound of B and O ....

c a compound of C and S ....

d the simplest compound of N and H. ....

Practice

4 Lactose (a sugar), $C_{12}H_{22}O_{11}$, is sometimes used instead of charcoal in fireworks. State the total number of atoms present in a molecule of lactose.

....

5 Atoms of elements P, Q and R have 16, 17 and 19 electrons, respectively. The atoms of argon have 18 electrons.

Predict the formulae of the compounds formed by the combination of the elements:

a P and R ....

b Q and R ....

c Q with itself. ....

In each of the three cases shown in **a–c**, name the type of chemical bond formed.

d **i** ....

ii ....

iii ....

Challenge

6 Write the formulae of the following ionic compounds and state which ions are present in each compound. Use information from your completed Periodic Table in Figure 3.1.

a a compound of Mg and Br

....

KEY WORDS

molecular formula: a formula that shows the actual number of atoms of each element present in a molecule of a compound.

state symbols: symbols used to show the physical state of the reactants and products in a chemical reaction: they are s (solid), l (liquid), g (gas) and aq (in solution in water).

word equation: a summary of a chemical reaction using the chemical names of the reactants and products.

TIP

Some elements normally exist as diatomic molecules. You can remember the symbols of these elements using this memory aid: I Have No **Br**ight Or **Cl**ever Friends.

b a compound of Ca and N

....

c a compound of Al and O

....

7 A molecule of compound Y contains the following atoms bonded covalently together:

- 2 atoms of carbon (C)
- 2 atoms of oxygen (O)
- 4 atoms of hydrogen (H).

What is the molecular formula of a molecule of Y?...

8 Use the words provided to complete the paragraphs about the formulae of compounds. Some words may be used more than once.

atoms   bonded   carbon   compound

hydrogen   ionic   molecular   ratio

The formula of a simple molecular _____ shows exactly how many

atoms are _____ together in each molecule. For example, ethane has two

_____ and six _____ atoms, so its formula is C_2H_6. This is the

_____ formula for ethane.

The formulae used for giant covalent and _____ compounds are the

simplest _____ of the different _____ or ions in each compound.

Exercise 3.2

IN THIS EXERCISE YOU WILL:

- write word equations and balanced chemical (symbol) equations for chemical reactions
- use state symbols to add to the information given in an equation
- construct formulae, from ions, in which the charges balance so that the overall formula has no charge
- convert symbol equations into ionic equations to show the ions taking part in a reaction.

Focus

1   The 'model equation' in Figure 3.2 describes the combustion of methane.

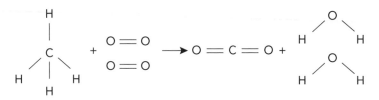

Figure 3.2: The combustion of methane.

a   Write the word equation for this reaction.

....

b   Write the balanced chemical (symbol) equation for this reaction.

....

c   Add the state symbols to your answer to part **b**.

2   Write word equations for the following reactions:

a $Zn + CuSO_4 \rightarrow ZnSO_4 + Cu$

....

b $NH_4Cl + NaOH \rightarrow NH_3 + NaCl + H_2O$

....

c $4Fe + 3O_2 \rightarrow 2Fe_2O_3$

....

3   Balance the following symbol equations:

a   ....Na + ...Cl_2 → ....NaCl

b   ....SO_2 + ...O_2 → ....SO_3

c   ....Fe_2O_3 + ...CO → ....Fe + ...CO_2

d   ....PbO + ...C → ....Pb + ...CO_2

> **TIP**
>
> When balancing symbol equations, do not change any of the formulae of the substances involved. Always balance by putting whole numbers in front of the formulae.

Practice

4 Table 3.1 shows the valencies and formulae of some common ions.

		Valency		
		1	2	3
Positive ions (cations)	metals	sodium (Na⁺) potassium (K⁺) silver (Ag⁺)	magnesium (Mg²⁺) copper (Cu²⁺) zinc (Zn²⁺) iron (Fe²⁺)	aluminium (Al³⁺) iron (Fe³⁺) chromium (Cr³⁺)
	compound ions	ammonium (NH₄⁺)		
Negative ions (anions)	non-metals	choride (Cl⁻) bromide (Br⁻) iodide (I⁻)	oxide (O²⁻) sulphide (S²⁻)	nitride (N³⁻)
	compound ions	nitrate (NO₃⁻) hydroxide (OH⁻)	carbonate (CO₃²⁻) sulfate (SO₄²⁻)	phosphate (PO₄³⁻)

Table 3.1: Valencies and formulae of some common ions.

Use the information in the table to work out the formulae of the following ionic compounds:

a copper(II) oxide ....

b sodium carbonate ....

c zinc(II) sulfate ....

d silver(I) nitrate ....

e ammonium sulfate ....

f potassium phosphate ....

g iron(III) hydroxide ....

h chromium(III) chloride ....

5 Use the information in Table 3.1 and your answers to question 4 to give the ratio of the different atoms in the following compounds.

a copper(II) oxide, Cu : O ....

b iron(III) hydroxide, Fe : O : H ....

c ammonium sulfate, N : H : S : O. ....

6   Figure 3.3 is a representation of the structure of an ionic oxide.

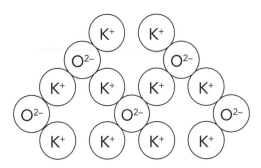

Figure 3.3: Structure of an ionic oxide.

> **TIP**
>
> When writing a formula of an ionic compound from a diagram of the structure, make sure you write the simplest ratio of the ions present.

a   What is the ratio of K⁺ ions to O²⁻ ions? ....

b   What is the formula of this compound? ....

Challenge

7   Figure 3.4 shows the structure of common salt.

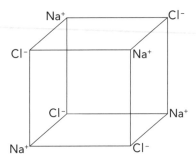

Figure 3.4: Structure of common salt.

a   Add four more ions to extend the structure in Figure 3.4 to the right.

b   Complete Figure 3.5a and b to show the electronic configuration of the ions in the structure. Draw any missing electron shells, clearly showing the origin of the electrons involved.

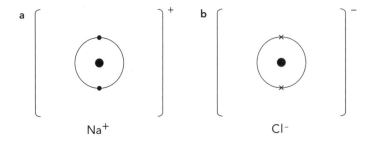

Figure 3.5: The electronic configuration of **a:** a sodium ion and **b:** a chloride ion.

8 Convert these equations into ionic equations:

a $Cl_2(aq) + 2KBr(aq) \rightarrow 2KCl(aq) + Br_2(aq)$

....

b $Mg(s) + 2HCl(aq) \rightarrow MgCl_2(aq) + H_2(g)$

....

c $FeCl_2(aq) + 2NaOH(aq) \rightarrow Fe(OH)_2(s) + 2NaCl(aq)$

....

d $ZnCl_2(aq) + Mg(s) \rightarrow MgCl_2(aq) + Zn(s)$

....

> Relative masses of atoms and molecules

Exercise 3.3

IN THIS EXERCISE YOU WILL:

- use relative atomic mass to calculate the relative molecular or formula masses of compounds

- understand how relative molecular masses can be used to calculate the proportions of reactants and products

- develop your skills in processing and interpreting results from practical work

- show how experimental data can be used to find the proportions of reactants and products.

KEY WORDS

relative atomic mass (A_r): the average mass of naturally occurring atoms of an element on a scale where an atom of carbon-12 has a mass of 12 exactly.

relative formula mass (M_r): the sum of all the relative atomic masses of the atoms present in a 'formula unit' of a substance.

relative molecular mass (M_r): the sum of all the relative atomic masses of the atoms present in a molecule.

Focus

1 Complete Figure 3.6 by filling in the blanks.

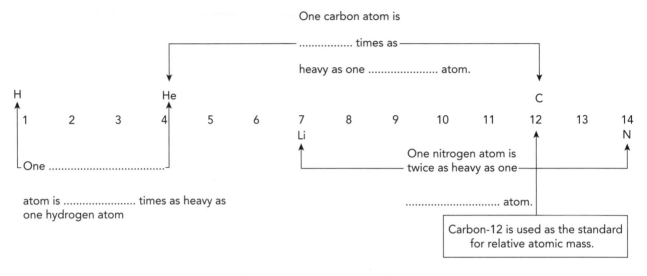

Figure 3.6: Relative atomic mass.

2 Zinc metal is extracted from its oxide. In the industrial extraction process, 5 tonnes of zinc oxide are needed to produce 4 tonnes of zinc. Calculate the mass of zinc, in tonnes, that is produced from 20 tonnes of zinc oxide.

....

....

3 When ammonia burns in oxygen, the following reaction takes place. The masses reacting are given along with the mass of nitrogen formed:

$$4NH_3 + 3O_2 \rightarrow 2N_2 + 6H_2O$$

68 g   96 g   56 g

a What mass of water is formed in this reaction?

....

....

b What mass of water is formed if 17 g of ammonia is burnt?

....

....

Practice

4   Complete Table 3.2, which shows the relative molecular (or formula) masses for a
range of different substances.

(Relative atomic masses: O = 16, H = 1, C = 12, N = 14, Ca = 40, Mg = 24)

Molecule	Chemical formula	Number of atoms or ions involved	Relative molecular (or formula) mass
oxygen	O_2	2O	2 × 16 = 32
carbon dioxide		1C and 2O	1 × 12 + 2 × 16 = _____
	H_2O	2H and 1O	_____ = _____
ammonia		1N and 3H	_____ = _____
calcium carbonate		$1Ca^{2+}$ and $1CO_3^{2-}$	_____ + _____ + 3 × 16 = 100
	MgO	$1Mg^{2+}$ and $1O^{2-}$	1 × 24 + 1 × 16 = _____
ammonium nitrate	NH_4NO_3	$1NH_4^+$ and _____	2 × 14 + _____ + _____ = 80
propanol	C_3H_7OH	3C, _____ and _____	3 × 12 + 8 × 1 + _____ = _____

Table 3.2: Some relative molecular (or formula) masses.

Challenge

5 Magnesium oxide is made when magnesium is burnt in air. A student wants to find out how the mass of magnesium oxide made depends on the mass of magnesium burnt.

The practical method is as follows.

Method

- Weigh an empty crucible and lid.

- Roll some magnesium ribbon around a pencil, place it in the crucible and re-weigh (including the lid).

- Place the crucible in a pipeclay triangle sitting safely on a tripod. The lid should be on the crucible.

- Heat the crucible and its contents strongly, as shown in Figure 3.7. Lift the lid occasionally to allow more air in.

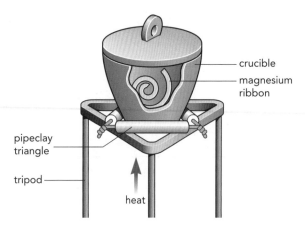

Figure 3.7: Heating magnesium ribbon.

- When the reaction has eased, take off the lid.

- Heat strongly for another three minutes.

- Let the crucible cool down and then weigh it.

- Repeat the heating until the mass is constant.

Results

A class of students completed this experiment. Table 3.3 shows the students' results.

Mass of magnesium / g	0.06	0.05	0.04	0.18	0.16	0.10	0.11	0.14	0.15	0.14	0.08	0.10	0.13
Mass of magnesium oxide / g	0.10	0.08	0.06	0.28	0.25	0.15	0.15	0.21	0.24	0.23	0.13	0.17	0.21

Table 3.3: Results for burning magnesium in air.

a Use these results to plot a graph on the grid provided, relating the mass of magnesium oxide made to the mass of magnesium used. Remember there is one point on this graph that you can be certain of. Think carefully what that point should be and include it on your graph. Then answer the questions based on these results.

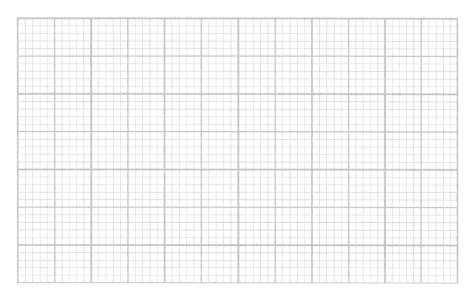

b How does the mass of magnesium oxide depend on the starting mass of magnesium?

....

c Use the graph to work out the mass of magnesium oxide that would be produced from 0.12 g of magnesium. Show the lines you use for this on your graph.

.................g

d What mass of oxygen combines with 0.12 g of magnesium? ....g

e What mass of oxygen combines with 24 g of magnesium? ....g

f If you heated 3.5 g of magnesium in a crucible, how much magnesium oxide would be formed? (Assume the reaction goes to completion.)

....

....

g Would magnesium oxide be the only product formed in this reaction? Suggest another possible product and give the formula of that product.

....

> The mole and the Avogadro Constant

Exercise 3.4

IN THIS EXERCISE YOU WILL:

- apply the concept of the mole to industrial-scale reacting amounts

- use calculation triangles as a memory aid in calculations on the mole.

Focus

In the laboratory, you will be used to working with grams of material and your calculations will be framed on that basis. However, an industrial chemist will work on a significantly larger scale; they might be looking to produce tonnes of product.

1   You can use the equation for a reaction to determine the proportions of the substances reacting. These proportions can be scaled up to provide useful data at an industrial level.

   a   What mass of iron(III) oxide is needed to produce 100 g of iron, in the blast furnace?

$$(A_r: C = 12; O = 16; Fe = 56)$$

The equation for the reaction is:

$$Fe_2O_3(s) + 3CO(g) \rightarrow 2Fe(s) + 3CO_2(g)$$

....

....

....

TIP

Remember that one tonne (a metric ton) = 1000 kilograms.

KEY WORDS

mass concentration: the measure of the concentration of a solution in terms of the mass of the solute, in grams, dissolved per cubic decimetre of solution (g/dm^3).

molar gas volume: 1 mole of any gas has the same volume under the same conditions of temperature and pressure ($24 dm^3$ at r.t.p.).

mole: the measure of amount of substance in chemistry; 1 mole of a substance has a mass equal to its relative formula mass in grams; that amount of substance contains 6.02×10^{23} (the Avogadro constant) atoms, molecules or formula units depending on the substance considered.

r.t.p.: room temperature and pressure: the standard values are 25 °C (298 K) and 101.3 kPa (1 atmosphere pressure).

b Complete the following sentence using your calculated figures.

100 g of iron is _____ moles of Fe, so _____ moles of Fe_2O_3 are needed for the reaction. This is _____ g of iron(III) oxide.

c State how much iron(III) oxide (hematite) is needed to produce 50 tonnes of iron. Use your calculated value for the amount of hematite needed to produce 100 g of iron.

....

....

2 Another large-scale industrial process is the production of quicklime (calcium oxide, CaO) from limestone by heating in a lime kiln.

a What is the equation for the thermal decomposition of limestone?

....

b Using your equation, calculate how many tonnes of quicklime (calcium oxide, CaO) would be produced from 1 tonne of limestone. (A_r: Ca = 40)

....

....

....

Practice

3 The mathematical equation that relates the mass of a substance (in g) to the number of moles present is:

$$\text{number of moles} = \frac{\text{mass}}{\text{molar mass}}$$

If you know two of these values, you can calculate the third by rearranging the equation. You can set up a calculation triangle to check that you have rearranged the equation correctly.

a Fill in the calculation triangle in Figure 3.8, for changing between masses and moles.

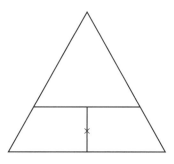

Figure 3.8: Calculation triangle for converting mass to moles.

b Now use the calculation triangle to complete Table 3.4.

(A_r: H = 1, C = 12, N = 14, O = 16, Mg = 24, S = 32, Cl = 35.5, Ca = 40, Cu = 64)

Substance	A_r or M_r	Number of moles	Mass/g
Cu			128.0
Mg		0.5	
Cl_2			35.5
H_2			4.0
S_8		2.0	
O_3			1.6
H_2SO_4		2.5	
CO_2		0.4	
NH_3			25.5
$CaCO_3$			100.0

Table 3.4: Calculations between moles and mass of substance.

Challenge

4 **a** Use your answer from the first row of Table 3.4 to calculate the number of atoms present in 128 g of copper.

....

....

b Calculate the number of hydrogen atoms present in 4 g of hydrogen gas. Use the information in Table 3.4.

....

....

c   Use Table 3.4 to work out the formula of copper(II) nitrate. Then use this formula to calculate the mass of 7.4 moles of copper(II) nitrate.

....

....

Exercise 3.5

IN THIS EXERCISE YOU WILL:

• convert the mass of a substance into moles

• consider the relationship between volume and the number of moles of a gas.

Focus

As for conversion between mass and moles, we can use a triangle to help us when calculating volumes of a gas.

1   Complete the triangle in Figure 3.9 to show how you can convert between moles, molar volume and volume of a gas at room temperature and pressure (r.t.p.).

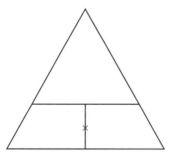

Figure 3.9: Calculation triangle for converting moles of a gas.

2   Use the triangle in Figure 3.9 to calculate the volume of 2.3 moles of oxygen.

....

....

3 A reaction produces $17\,g$ of CO_2. What volume will this occupy?

....

....

Practice

A student reacts $24\,g$ of magnesium with excess sulfuric acid. They use the chemical equation for the reaction, the relative formula masses of the substances and the molar gas volume to predict the amounts of magnesium sulfate and hydrogen produced.

$$Mg \quad + \quad H_2SO_4 \quad \rightarrow \quad MgSO_4 \quad + \quad H_2$$

Mg	H₂SO₄	MgSO₄	H₂
24 g	excess	120 g	24 000 cm³

The relationship between the mass of magnesium used and the volume of gas produced can be used to find the mass of a short piece of magnesium ribbon indirectly.

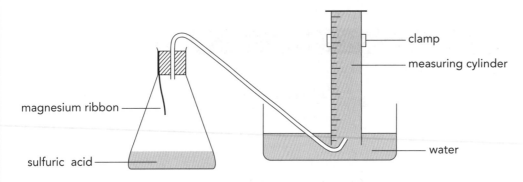

Figure 3.10: Experimental setup to find the mass of a piece of magnesium ribbon.

The experimental instructions are as follows:

- Wear safety goggles for eye protection.

- Set up the apparatus as shown in Figure 3.10, with $25\,cm^3$ of sulfuric acid in the flask.

- Make sure the measuring cylinder is completely full of water.

- Carefully measure $5\,cm$ of magnesium ribbon and use the flask stopper to grip the ribbon as shown.

- Ease the stopper up to release the ribbon and immediately replace the stopper.

- When no further bubbles rise into the measuring cylinder, record the volume of gas collected.

- Repeat the experiment twice more. Use 5 cm of magnesium ribbon and fresh sulfuric acid each time.
- Find the mean average volume of hydrogen produced.

A student measured the volume of hydrogen produced. They obtained the results shown in Table 3.5.

Experiment number	Volume of hydrogen collected / cm³
1	85
2	79
3	82
Mean average	

Table 3.5: Experimental results: volume of hydrogen produced.

4 Calculate the mean average of the results obtained in the table above. Use the space in Table 3.5 to write your answer. In the space below, can you think of possible reasons why the three results are not the same?

....

....

....

5 You know that 24 g of magnesium will produce 24 000 cm³ of hydrogen at r.t.p. Calculate the mass of magnesium needed to produce your volume of hydrogen.

....

....

6 What mass of magnesium sulfate would you expect 5 cm of magnesium ribbon to produce?

....

....

7 Plan an experiment to check whether your prediction in question 6 is correct.

....

....

....

....

....

....

....

....

....

....

Challenge

Experiments show that volumes of gases react together in a ratio that can be predicted from the chemical equation for a reaction.

Under the conditions used here, nitrogen monoxide (NO) reacts with oxygen (O_2) to form one product that is a brown gas. In an experiment, $5\,cm^3$ portions of oxygen were pushed from syringe B into syringe A (Figure 3.11).

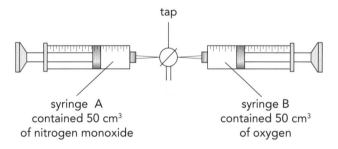

syringe A
contained 50 cm³
of nitrogen monoxide

syringe B
contained 50 cm³
of oxygen

Figure 3.11: Syringe apparatus for a gas experiment.

After each addition, the tap was closed and the gases were cooled. Then the total volume of gases remaining was measured. The results are shown in Figure 3.12.

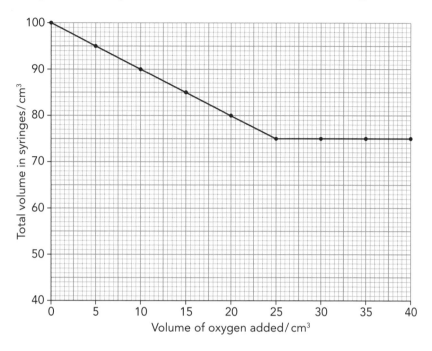

Figure 3.12: Graph of experimental results.

8 What is the total volume of gases when the reaction is complete?

....

9 What volume of oxygen reacts with 50 cm³ of nitrogen monoxide?

....

10 What is the volume of the brown gas formed?

....

11 Complete the following to work out the formula of the brown gas:

.... NO   +   O₂   →   ....

50 cm³   .... cm³   .... cm³

> Chapter 4
Electrochemistry

> ## Electrolysis
Exercise 4.1

IN THIS EXERCISE YOU WILL:

- describe how metals are electrical conductors and non-metallic materials are non-conducting insulators
- consider the process of electrolysis
- learn how to describe the electrode products of electrolysis
- learn that, in electrolysis, the positive electrode is known as the anode and the negative electrode is known as the cathode
- link the properties of ionic compounds to their structure and bonding.

KEY WORDS

anode: the positive electrode in electrolysis.

cathode: the negative electrode in electrolysis.

electrodes: the points where the electric current enters or leaves a battery or electrolytic cell.

electrolysis: the breakdown of an ionic compound by the use of electricity; the compound must be molten or in aqueous solution (dissolved in water).

electrolyte: an ionic compound that will conduct electricity when it is molten or dissolved in water; electrolytes will not conduct electricity when solid.

Focus

1   Figure 4.1 shows an electrolytic cell that could be used to test whether a liquid substance or aqueous solution conducts electricity by electrolysis.

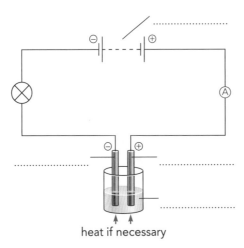

heat if necessary

Figure 4.1: Electrolytic cell for testing the electrical conductivity of a liquid or solution. Heat can be supplied if necessary.

a   Complete Figure 4.1 by labelling the electrolyte, the anode, the cathode and the power supply.

b   Name *two* substances that are often used as inert electrodes in an electrolytic cell like this.

....

KEY WORDS

electrolytic cell: a cell consisting of an electrolyte and two electrodes (anode and cathode) connected to an external DC power source where positive and negative ions in the electrolyte are separated and discharged.

Practice

2   Complete the following statements about electrical conductivity and electrolysis by linking the phrases A to D on the left with the phrases 1 to 4 on the right.

A Sulfur does not conduct electricity …	**1** … because the ions present are in fixed positions in the structure and not free to move.
B Solid lead(II) bromide does not conduct electricity …	**2** … because there are free delocalised electrons in the structure that are free to move.
C Metallic elements and alloys conduct electricity …	**3** … because none of the electrons in the structure are free to move.
D Molten lead(II) bromide conducts electricity …	**4** … because the ions present in the molten liquid are free to move.

Challenge

3   Describe why molten ionic compounds and aqueous solutions of ionic compounds conduct electricity while solid ionic compounds do not. Refer to the structure and bonding present (see Chapter 2).

....

....

....

....

....

....

Exercise 4.2

IN THIS EXERCISE YOU WILL:

- describe the terms anion (positive ion) and cation (negative ion) in relation to the direction of ion movement during electrolysis

- consider the products of electrolysis of molten binary compounds

- consider the products of electrolysis of aqueous compounds.

TIP

During electrolysis, metals or hydrogen are formed at the cathode and non-metals (other than hydrogen) are formed at the anode.

Focus

1   Crystals of ionic compounds do not conduct electricity. However, when the crystals are melted the molten liquid allows a current to flow. A chemical reaction takes place in which the ionic salt is broken down (decomposed) into its elements.

Table 4.1 lists four molten binary compounds. Complete the table by stating the electrode products following electrolysis. Complete the final column of the table with observations of the product given off at the anode.

Molten electrolyte	Product at anode (+)	Product at cathode (−)	Observations of product at anode
lead(II) iodide			
magnesium chloride			
zinc bromide			
calcium oxide			

Table 4.1: Products and observations following electrolysis of molten ionic compounds.

Practice

2   A student set up an experiment to show the movement of ions in solution (see Figure 4.2).

The filter paper is damp. A small crystal of the solid being studied is placed in the centre of the filter paper as shown.

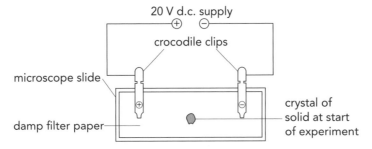

Figure 4.2: Experiment to show the movement of ions in an electric field.

The results of the experiment are shown in Table 4.2.

Substance	Colour of crystals	Changes seen on the filter paper
potassium chromate, K_2CrO_4	yellow	yellow colour moves towards positive
potassium sulfate, K_2SO_4	white	no colours seen
copper(II) sulfate, $CuSO_4$	blue	blue colour moves towards negative

Table 4.2: Results from an experiment to show the movement of ions in an electric field.

a   Which of these ions is yellow? Circle the correct answer.

        chromate   copper   potassium   sulfate

b   Explain why the yellow colour moves towards the positive terminal in the potassium chromate experiment.

....

....

c   Suggest and explain what will happen if this experiment is repeated with copper chromate.

....

....

....

....

PEER ASSESSMENT

Discuss your answers to question **3c** with a partner. What is the difference between the command words 'suggest' and 'explain'? Have you suggested what will happen and explained why in your answer?

Challenge

3   Use the words provided to complete the following text. Some words may be used more than once.

anode   cathode   current   electrodes   electrolyte   hydrogen

hydroxide   lose   molecules   molten   positive   solution

During electrolysis, ionic compounds are broken down (decomposed) by the passage of an electric current. For this to happen, the compound must be either _____ or in _____ in water.

Electrolysis can occur when an electric _____ passes through a molten _____. The two rods dipping into the electrolyte are called the _____. In this situation, metals are deposited at the _____ and non-metals are formed at the _____.

When the ionic compound is dissolved in water, the electrolysis can be more complex. Generally, during electrolysis, _____ ions move towards the _____ and negative ions move towards the _____. At the negative electrode (cathode), the metal or _____ ions gain electrons, forming metal atoms or hydrogen _____. At the positive electrode (anode), non-metals are formed as their ions or _____ ions from the water _____ electrons.

Exercise 4.3

IN THIS EXERCISE YOU WILL:

- consider the electrolysis of molten and aqueous solutions
- predict the products of electrolysis using data provided
- write half-equations for the reactions at the electrodes.

Focus

1   An electrolytic cell can be used to decompose both aqueous solutions and molten compounds.

Complete Table 4.3 to identify the ions, products and observations during electrolysis of molten lead(II) bromide and dilute sulfuric acid.

Electrolyte	molten lead(II) bromide	dilute sulfuric acid
Ions present in solution		
Product at the anode		
Product at the cathode		
Observations during electrolysis		

Table 4.3: Electrolysis of molten lead(II) bromide and dilute sulfuric acid.

Practice

2   Table 4.4 shows the results of electrolysis of some aqueous solutions using inert electrodes. Use the information in the top part of the table to fill in the gaps. All the solutions were electrolysed under exactly the same conditions.

Solution (electrolyte)	Gas given off at anode	Gas given off or metal deposited at cathode	Substance left in solution at the end of electrolysis
copper(II) sulfate	oxygen	copper	sulfuric acid
sodium sulfate	oxygen	hydrogen	sodium sulfate
concentrated sodium chloride	chlorine	hydrogen	sodium hydroxide
silver nitrate	oxygen	silver	nitric acid
concentrated potassium bromide		hydrogen	
copper(II) nitrate		copper	nitric acid
silver sulfate	oxygen		
sodium nitrate		hydrogen	sodium nitrate

Table 4.4: The electrolysis of aqueous solutions using inert electrodes.

Challenge

3   In question 1, you completed Table 4.3 using the example of molten lead(II) bromide and dilute sulfuric acid. Now complete Table 4.5 to show the half-equations for this electrolysis.

Electrolyte	molten lead(II) bromide	dilute sulfuric acid
Half-equation at anode		
Half-equation at cathode		

Table 4.5: Half-equations for electrolysis of molten lead(II) bromide and dilute sulfuric acid.

Exercise 4.4

IN THIS EXERCISE YOU WILL:

- describe what happens during electrolysis

- investigate the electrolysis of copper(II) chloride solution using carbon electrodes

- learn how changing the nature of the electrodes alters the products formed during electrolysis.

Focus

1   Copper(II) chloride can be decomposed to its elements by electrolysis of a solution of the salt. A simple cell can be set up so that the chlorine gas can be collected (Figure 4.3).

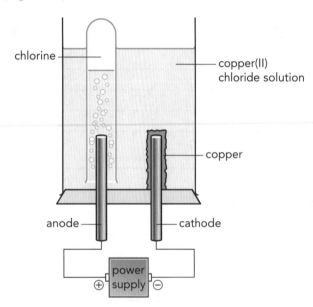

Figure 4.3: Electrolysis of copper(II) chloride solution.

a   Write the word and balanced symbol equations for the overall reaction taking place during this electrolysis.

....

....

b   The mass of the cathode was found to increase during this experiment.
Explain this observation.

....

....

Practice

2   Figure 4.4 shows the electrolytic cell used in the electrolysis of copper(II) sulfate
solution using copper electrodes.

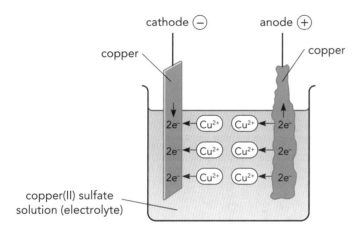

Figure 4.4: The electrolysis of copper(II) sulfate solution using copper electrodes.

a   Use information from Figure 4.4 to write half-equations for the reactions
taking place at the anode and at the cathode in this electrolysis.

....

....

b   Predict the change in mass of the copper electrodes that could be detected if
the electrolysis was carried out for a sufficient period of time.

i   Change in mass of the cathode: ....

....

....

ii   Change in mass of the anode: ....

....

....

Challenge

3 Explain why the colour of the copper(II) sulfate solution does not change during the electrolysis.

....

....

....

....

> Hydrogen–oxygen fuel cells

Exercise 4.5

IN THIS EXERCISE YOU WILL:

- review the basic features of electrolysis

- investigate how a hydrogen–oxygen fuel cell can be used to power vehicles

- consider the advantages and disadvantages of hydrogen–oxygen fuel cells.

KEY WORD

fuel cell: a device for continuously converting chemical energy into electrical energy using a combustion reaction; a hydrogen fuel cell uses the reaction between hydrogen and oxygen.

Focus

1 Figure 4.5 shows a hydrogen–oxygen fuel cell in a car. Add labels to the arrows going into and coming out from the fuel cell to show the reactants and products. Take care to identify the anode and the cathode.

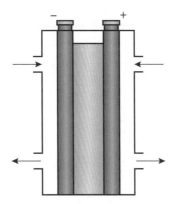

Figure 4.5: A hydrogen–oxygen fuel cell in a car.

Practice

2   Hydrogen–oxygen fuel cells can be used to provide energy for vehicles. They have some advantages and some disadvantages when used in this way.

  a   Give *two* advantages of using hydrogen–oxygen fuel cells to power vehicles.

....

....

  b   Suggest *two* practical problems that will need to be overcome before hydrogen–oxygen fuel cells can be used in a fully carbon-neutral road transport system.

....

....

Challenge

3   Figure 4.6 shows the basic structure of a hydrogen–oxygen fuel cell.

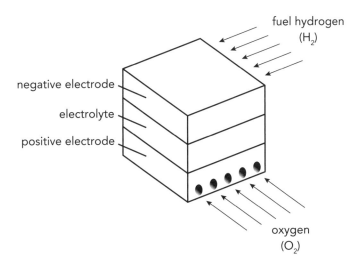

Figure 4.6: The structure of a hydrogen–oxygen fuel cell.

  a   Hydrogen gas enters the cell at the negative electrode and is converted into hydrogen (H^+) ions. Write the ionic half-equation for this electrode reaction.

....

b In a hydrogen fuel cell with an acidic electrolyte, oxygen enters the cell and reacts with the hydrogen ions in the electrolyte to produce water. Balance the electrode half-equation for this reaction.

$O_2(g) +$ _____ $H^+(aq) +$ _____ $e^- \rightarrow$ _____ $H_2O(l)$

c Add together the half-equations from a and b to give the overall reaction.

....

> **TIP**
>
> Half-equations are ionic equations that show the individual reactions at the anode (oxidation) and cathode (reduction) in an electrochemical cell. Half-equations are balanced when each side is neutral.

Chapter 5

Chemical energetics

> Exothermic and endothermic reactions

Exercise 5.1

IN THIS EXERCISE YOU WILL:

- look at the properties of exothermic and endothermic changes
- investigate the uses of these types of change
- consider how an exothermic or endothermic reaction can be followed practically
- interpret the results from a practical investigation of a chemical reaction in which an energy change takes place.

Focus

1   Draw lines between the two columns to show which statements are true for exothermic and endothermic reactions.

Type of reaction	Statement / fact
exothermic	the temperature decreases
	heat energy is given out to the surroundings
	the temperature increases
endothermic	combustion is an example of this type of reaction
	heat energy is taken in from the surroundings

KEY WORDS

activation energy (E_a): the minimum energy required to start a chemical reaction; for a reaction to take place, the colliding particles must possess at least this amount of energy.

endothermic change: a process or chemical reaction which takes in heat from the surroundings.

exothermic change: a process or chemical reaction in which heat energy is produced and released to the surroundings.

reaction level diagram (energy pathway diagram): a diagram that shows the energy levels of the reactants and products in a chemical reaction; it shows whether a reaction is exothermic or endothermic.

Practice

2 The reaction between calcium oxide (slaked lime) and water can be used to heat up drinks such as coffee and tea. When this reaction takes place, a great deal of heat is given off and the solid calcium oxide swells to occupy a greater volume.

Figure 5.1 shows one way of constructing a self-heating drinks can.

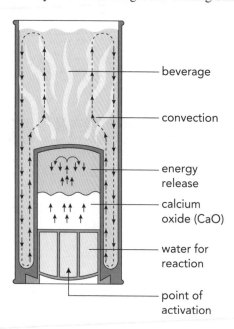

Figure 5.1: A self-heating drinks can.

a What term is used for a reaction that gives out heat to the external surroundings?

....

b What problem might occur because of the expansion of the solid when water is added?

....

c Look carefully at Figure 5.1 and suggest how this problem might be overcome.

....

d Write the word and balanced symbol equations for the reaction between calcium oxide and water to give calcium hydroxide.

....

....

Challenge

3 Reactions that absorb heat from the surroundings can be used to cool things down or keep them cool. Figure 5.2 shows two types of cool pack.

- Instant cool packs contain a solid which dissolves endothermically in water. The water and the solid are kept separate until the cooling effect is needed.

- Other cool packs contain a gel which is cooled down in a freezer and then warms up slowly when removed. This type of cool pack can be reused.

Figure 5.2: Two types of cool pack.

Instant cool packs usually contain crystals of ammonium nitrate together with a plastic bag of water. The bag of water is burst to activate the pack.

a Give *one* advantage and *one* disadvantage of this type of cool pack.

advantage: ....

disadvantage: ....

b Cool packs can be used to keep vaccines and other medicines cool in hot climates. For this purpose, a temperature of 5°C is usually required.

You are asked to find the mass of ammonium nitrate that could be used with 10cm³ of water to make a cool pack for medicines that can cool to 5°C.

Briefly describe a plan for carrying out this investigation. In your plan:

- Name the apparatus you would use.
- Give the variables you would control to make it a fair test. (Remember that everything should be the same except the thing you are testing.)
- Describe how you would carry out the experiment.
- Identify the measurements you would take.
- Explain how you would use your results to find the answer to the problem.

....

....

....

....

....

....

....

TIP

In your experiment, you are unlikely to choose a mass of ammonium nitrate that gives a temperature change of exactly 5°C. Think about how you can use a graph to help you find the answer.

Exercise 5.2

IN THIS EXERCISE YOU WILL:

- interpret reaction pathway diagrams for exothermic and endothermic reactions
- describe bond-making as exothermic and bond-breaking as endothermic.

Focus

1   The energy changes involved in chemical reactions can be represented visually by reaction pathway (or energy level) diagrams. These diagrams show the relative energy of the reactants and products.

a   Cross out the incorrect words in the following paragraph. Use Figure 5.3 to help you.

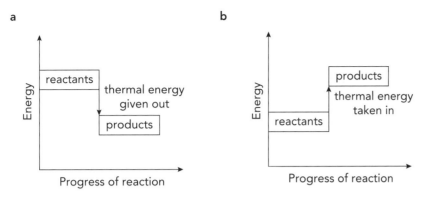

TIP

When you measure the temperature of the reaction mixture, you measure the temperature of the surroundings, not of the reaction itself.

Figure 5.3: Reaction pathway diagrams for **a:** an exothermic reaction and **b:** an endothermic reaction.

In an exothermic reaction, the **reactants / products** have more thermal energy than the **reactants / products**. This means that **thermal energy / potential energy** is transferred **to / from** the surroundings. As a result, the temperature of the surroundings **increases / decreases**.

In an endothermic reaction, the **reactants / products** have more thermal energy than the **reactants / products**. This means that energy is transferred **to / from** the surroundings and the temperature of the surroundings **increases / decreases**.

The enthalpy change, ΔH, of a reaction is a measure of the **thermal / potential** energy change during a reaction. For an exothermic reaction, ΔH is **negative / positive**. For an endothermic reaction, ΔH is **negative / positive**.

b Use the words provided to complete the following paragraph.

broken   endothermic   exothermic   given out

made   taken in   formed

When bonds are _____, energy has to be added to the system and so

the reaction is _____. When bonds are _____, energy is given

out by the system and so the reaction is _____.

The enthalpy change for a reaction is the difference between the energy

_____ when bonds are broken and the energy _____ when

bonds are _____.

Practice

2 The following equations show two chemical reactions, along with the energy change for each reaction.

$CH_4(g) + 2O_2(g) \rightarrow CO_2(g) + 2H_2O(l)$ (energy given out, temperature increases)

$CaCO_3(s) \xrightarrow{\text{heat}} CaO(s) + CO_2(g)$ (energy taken in, temperature decreases, overall energy from reaction = +178 kJ/mol)

a Use this information to complete the reaction pathway diagrams in Figure 5.4, by inserting the correct reactants (e.g. $CH_4 + 2O_2$) and products (e.g. $CO_2 + 2H_2O$).

Write the symbols for the reactants in the left-hand boxes. Write the symbols for the products in the right-hand boxes.

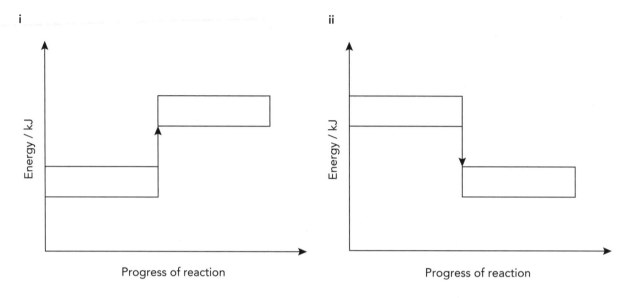

Figure 5.4: Reaction pathway diagrams.

b Label the enthalpy changes on each diagram, using the sign ΔH.

Challenge

3 Reaction pathway diagrams show how the energy changes during a reaction. Complete reaction pathway diagrams also include the activation energy (E_a). This is the energy required for the reaction to take place.

A complete reaction pathway diagram is shown in Figure 5.5.

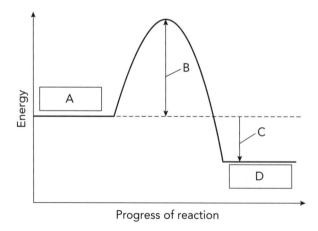

Figure 5.5: Reaction pathway diagram.

a Give the correct labels for A–D.

A ....

B ....

C ....

D ....

b Nitrogen and hydrogen react to form ammonia. This chemical reaction is extremely important in industry. The reaction is exothermic.

The equation for the reaction is shown, along with the activation energy (E_a):

$N_2(g) + 3H_2 \rightarrow 2NH_3(g)$ $E_a = +2000\,\text{kJ/mol}$

In the space, draw a reaction pathway diagram for this reaction.

- Draw and label the axes.

- Draw the expected reaction pathway for this reaction.

- Write the reactants and products in the correct places.

- Draw a labelled line to show the activation energy. Give the correct value.

- Draw a labelled line to show the enthalpy change. Use the sign ΔH.

PEER ASSESSMENT

Work with a partner. Write down *three* differences between the energy profiles for exothermic and endothermic reactions. Come up with a method to help you remember these differences. Then share your ideas with another pair.

> Chapter 6
Chemical reactions

> Physical and chemical changes

Exercise 6.1

IN THIS EXERCISE YOU WILL:

- identify physical and chemical changes and understand the differences between them
- use the criteria for identifying physical and chemical changes to classify different types of change.

KEY WORDS

chemical reaction (change): a change in which a new substance is formed.

physical change: a change in the physical state of a substance or the physical nature of a situation that does not involve a change in the chemical substance(s) present.

Focus

1   Use the words provided to complete the following paragraph. Words may be used once, more than once or not at all.

> **chemical   chemically   different   physical**
>
> **reverse   the same as   unchanged**

When a physical change takes place, the bonding within the substance undergoing

the change is _____ _____. When a _____ change takes

place, the substance or substances formed are _____ from the starting

substance.

_____ changes are easy to _____, so we can easily go back to the

starting substance. _____ changes are difficult to _____, so it is

more difficult to form the starting substance again.

Practice

2   Identify each of the following changes as a chemical or physical change.
Give *two* reasons for each answer.

   a   Ice melting

   ....

   ....

   ....

b Magnesium burning in air

....

....

....

c Salt dissolving in water

....

....

....

Challenge

3 When zinc carbonate ($ZnCO_3$) is heated strongly, the following observations are made:

- A colourless gas is given off which turns limewater cloudy.

- A solid is left that was yellow when hot and white when cold.

- When this cold solid was heated, it turned yellow again.

- This solid contained zinc and one other element.

a Complete the flowchart in Figure 6.1 by naming the chemicals in the boxes and writing the correct labels on the arrows.

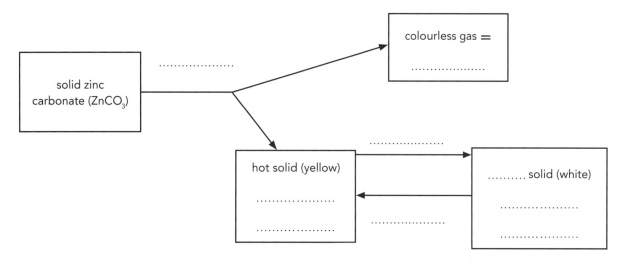

Figure 6.1: A flowchart of observations when zinc carbonate is heated strongly.

b Write the balanced symbol equation for the change taking place when the zinc carbonate is heated strongly.

....

c Is this a chemical or physical change? Explain your answer.

....

....

d Identify a physical change shown in the flowchart and explain your choice.

....

....

> Rate of reaction

Exercise 6.2

IN THIS EXERCISE YOU WILL:

- investigate what is meant by surface area and predict its effects on the rate of a chemical reaction

- look at an experiment to investigate the effect of surface area on reaction rate

- analyse the data from the experiment and plot a graph of the results

- use the results to deduce the effect of changing surface area on reaction rate.

Focus

1 Figure 6.2 shows:
   - a large piece of calcium carbonate (marble)
   - the same piece of calcium carbonate broken into smaller pieces.

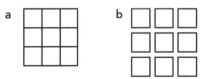

Figure 6.2: Calcium carbonate: a large piece **a** and broken into smaller pieces **b**.

KEY WORDS

catalyst: a substance that increases the rate of a chemical reaction but itself remains unchanged at the end of the reaction.

collision theory: a theory which states that a chemical reaction takes place when particles of the reactants collide with sufficient energy to initiate the reaction.

concentration: a measure of how much solute is dissolved in a solvent to make a solution. Solutions can be dilute (with a high proportion of the solvent) or concentrated (with a high proportion of the solute).

reaction rate: a measure of how fast a reaction takes place.

a Using the diagram, explain which of A or B has the greater surface area.

  ....

  ....

b When solid calcium carbonate reacts with hydrochloric acid and carbon
   dioxide, calcium chloride solution and water are formed.
   Write the word equation for this reaction, including state symbols.

  ....

We can use this reaction to investigate the effect of changing the surface area on the
rate of reaction. Carbon dioxide gas is given off, so the mass of the reaction mixture
changes. We can measure this change in mass using the apparatus shown in Figure 6.3.

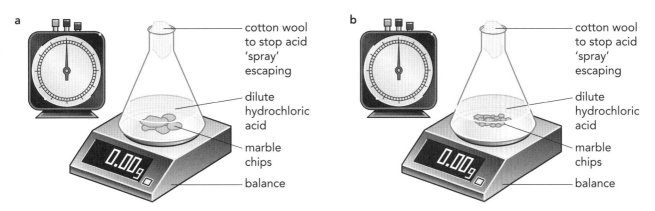

Figure 6.3: Experiment with **a:** large marble chips and acid and **b:** small marble chips and acid.

2 Does the mass measured on the balance increase or decrease in this reaction?
   Explain your answer.

  ....

  ....

Practice

3 To ensure the experiment gives a clear result, it must be a fair test. The only factor that is changed in the experiment shown in Figure 6.3 is the surface area of the calcium carbonate. Give *four* factors that must be kept constant (the same) in both experiments.

....

....

....

....

4 Choose *one* of these factors and explain its effect on the rate of reaction. Refer to collision theory in your answer.

....

....

....

5 Use the words provided to complete the following paragraph. Each word may be used once, more than once or not at all.

collide   connect   inside   outside   react

In the reaction between calcium carbonate and hydrochloric acid, the acid

particles can only collide and _____ with the calcium carbonate particles

on the _____ of the pieces. The calcium carbonate particles on the

_____ cannot react.

In the smaller pieces, the surface area is greater so more of the _____

particles are exposed to the acid. The acid particles can therefore _____

with more calcium carbonate particles and more reactions take place.

Challenge

Flask a contains larger pieces of marble chips and Flask b contains smaller pieces.

The change in mass of the flasks was recorded over time. Readings on the digital balance were taken every 30 seconds. The results are shown in Table 6.1.

Time/s	Flask a		Flask b	
	Mass/g	Loss in mass/g	Mass/g	Loss in mass/g
0	240.86	0.00	240.86	
30	240.65	0.21	240.35	
60	240.40	0.46	240.08	
90	240.21		239.99	
120	240.10		239.95	
150	240.05		239.92	
180	239.95		239.90	
210	239.94		239.88	
240	239.90		239.87	
270	239.88		239.86	
300	239.87		239.86	
330	239.86		239.86	
360	239.86		239.86	
390	239.86		239.86	
420	239.86		239.86	
450	239.86		239.86	

Table 6.1: Change in mass over time for flask a (larger pieces of marble chips) and flask b (smaller pieces of marble chips).

6   a   Fill in the gaps in the table by calculating the loss in mass at the different times. The first three have been done for you.

   b   Plot the two graphs for flasks a and b on the grid provided. Your graphs should satisfy the following requirements:

   • Use at least three-quarters of the grid.

   • Use different coloured points and lines for the two flasks.

   • Ensure each line is a smooth curve of best fit through the points.

   • The independent variable is time and the dependent variable is loss in mass.

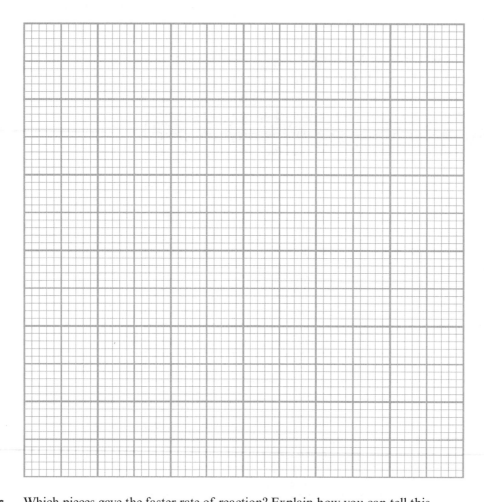

c Which pieces gave the faster rate of reaction? Explain how you can tell this from your graph.

....

....

....

7 a What does this experiment tell you about the effect of increasing surface area of a solid reactant on the rate of reaction?

....

b Explain why, for both flasks, the same amount of gas is produced at the end of the reaction.

....

Exercise 6.3

IN THIS EXERCISE YOU WILL:

- focus on what is meant by solution concentration and how it affects the rate of a reaction

- focus on what is meant by pressure and how it affects the rate of a reaction

- consider an experiment to find the effect of concentration on the rate of a reaction

- consider a graph to show how the production of a product varies with time

- predict the effects of changing concentration on the shapes of graphs

- predict and explain the effects of changing pressure on the rate of a reaction.

Focus

1   Cross out the incorrect words to complete the following sentences:

The concentration of a **solution / solvent** is a measure of the number of particles of **solute / solvent** per unit **volume / area**.

As we **increase / decrease** the pressure of a gas we increase the number of particles per unit **volume / area**.

2   Figure 6.4 shows three containers. The open circles represent water particles and the closed circles represent hydrochloric acid particles.

Complete the third box by drawing closed circles to represent the hydrochloric acid particles.

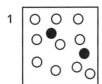
Volume = 1 dm³
Concentration = 1 mol / dm³

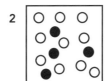
Volume = 1 dm³
Concentration = 2 mol / dm³

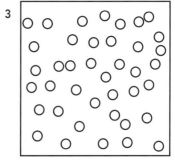
Volume = 4 dm³
Concentration = 1 mol / dm³

Figure 6.4: Particle diagrams showing water particles (open circles) and hydrochloric acid particles (closed circles).

Practice

3 **a** In the reaction between magnesium and hydrochloric acid solution,
the products are magnesium chloride (solution) and hydrogen gas.
Write the balanced symbol equation for the reaction.

....

b A student investigated the effect of changing the concentration of acid on the
rate of this reaction. The apparatus they used is shown in Figure 6.5.

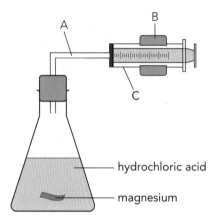

hydrochloric acid

magnesium

Figure 6.5: Apparatus to investigate the rate of reaction between magnesium and
hydrochloric acid solution.

Give the correct labels for A–C.

A ....

B ....

C ....

c What measurements would the student make when following the reaction?

....

4 In the Haber process, hydrogen and nitrogen gases are reacted together to form ammonia. This reaction can be carried out at high pressure using a pressure vessel.

Complete the diagram below to show the reactants at low pressure and at high pressure.

Low pressure

High pressure

Challenge

5 The student used 10 cm of magnesium ribbon for their experiments. Figure 6.6 shows the graph they obtained for the reaction with 1 mol/dm³ hydrochloric acid.

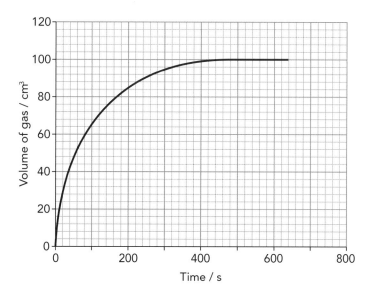

Figure 6.6: Graph to show the volume of hydrogen given off during the reaction of magnesium ribbon with hydrochloric acid.

a How long does it take to complete the reaction?

....

b Calculate the mean average rate of gas production for the reaction in cm³/s.

....

....

6 a On the axes in Figure 6.6, draw the graph expected if the concentration of hydrochloric acid was $2\,mol/dm^3$. Label the line you draw as X.

b On the axes in Figure 6.6, draw the line expected if the concentration of hydrochloric acid was $1\,mol/dm^3$ and the length of magnesium ribbon was reduced to 5 cm. Label the line you draw as Y.

c Draw a tangent to the curve X at 100 s and calculate the rate of the reaction at this time.

....

....

....

TIP
Calculate the slope of the tangent to find the rate of reaction.

d Explain why the rate of reaction decreases as the reaction proceeds.

....

....

....

7 As we increase the pressure of a gas, we increase the rate of reaction. Explain how this happens.

....

....

....

Exercise 6.4

Focus

1   The reaction between sodium thiosulfate and hydrochloric acid is described in the following word and symbol equations:

sodium thiosulfate (aq) + hydrochloric acid (aq) →   water (l)   + sulfur dioxide (g) + sulfur (s) + sodium chloride (aq)

……. $Na_2S_2O_3$ +   ……. $HCl(aq)$ → ……. $H_2O(l)$ +   ……. $SO_2(g)$ + ……. $S(s)$ +   ……. $NaCl(aq)$

    a   Balance the symbol equation.

    b   Explain why the reaction mixture turns cloudy as the reaction proceeds.

....

....

The method used to follow the course of the reaction is shown in Figure 6.7.

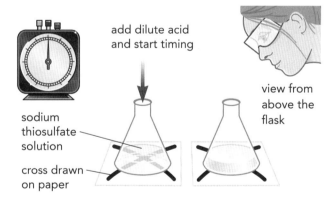

add dilute acid and start timing

view from above the flask

sodium thiosulfate solution

cross drawn on paper

Figure 6.7: The 'disappearing cross' experiment.

    c   Describe briefly how the method works.

....

....

d Comment on what safety precautions are needed and why.

....

....

....

Practice

2 Use the words provided to complete the following paragraph. Each word may be used once, more than once or not at all.

> **activation   collide   decreases   frequently   increases   kinetic**
>
> **less   more   potential   quickly   slowly   thermal**

When the temperature of a reaction mixture is increased, the particles have

more _____ energy and move around more _____. Because the

particles move around more _____ at higher temperatures, they collide

more _____ and this _____ the chance of a reaction taking

place. More importantly, when the particles do _____, the collisions are

_____ efficient. This means that more collisions have an energy greater

than the _____ energy (the energy required for a reaction to occur).

Challenge

3 Table 6.2 shows the results of experiments as shown in Figure 6.7, carried out at five different temperatures. In each case:

- 50 cm^3 of aqueous sodium thiosulfate was poured into a flask.

- 10 cm^3 of hydrochloric acid was added to the flask

- The initial and final temperatures were measured.

a   Use the thermometer diagrams to record the initial and final temperatures in Table 6.2. Complete the table to show the mean average temperatures.

Experiment	Thermometer diagram at start	Initial temperature / °C	Thermometer diagram at end	Final temperature / °C	Mean average temperature / °C	Time for cross to disappear / s
1	(30 / 25 / 20)		(30 / 25 / 20)			130
2	(40 / 35 / 30)		(40 / 35 / 30)			79
3	(45 / 40 / 35)		(45 / 40 / 35)			55
4	(55 / 50 / 45)		(55 / 50 / 45)			33
5	(60 / 55 / 50)		(60 / 55 / 50)			26

Table 6.2: Experimental results.

b On the grid provided, plot a graph of the time taken for the cross to disappear against the mean average temperature. Draw a smooth line to join the points.

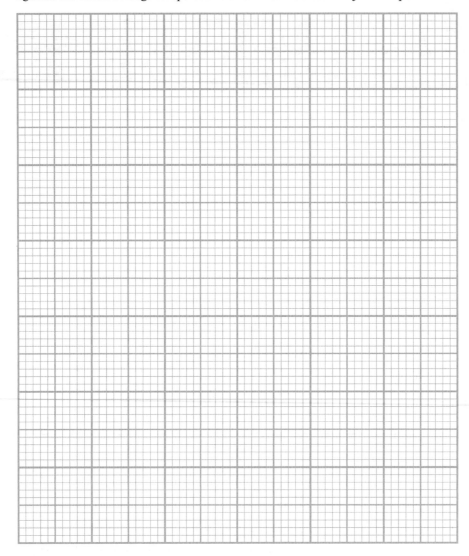

c In which experiment was the rate of reaction greatest? ....

d Explain why the rate was greatest in this experiment.

....

....

....

e Another way of following this reaction is by using a light data-logger.
The arrangement used is shown in Figure 6.8. Remember that the reaction
mixture becomes more cloudy as the reaction proceeds.

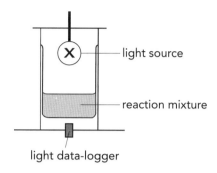

Figure 6.8: Using a light data-logger for the 'disappearing cross' experiment.

As the reaction proceeds, the reading on the light data-logger changes.
Explain why this happens.

....

....

....

....

f On the axes provided, draw the line you would expect for the reaction.

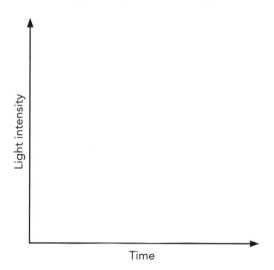

Exercise 6.5

IN THIS EXERCISE YOU WILL:

- design a procedure to show that a catalyst is unchanged in mass

- look at how a catalyst speeds up a chemical reaction

- look at reaction pathway diagrams to further explain the action of catalysts.

Focus

1   Manganese(IV) oxide is an insoluble black solid that catalyses the decomposition of hydrogen peroxide.

$$2H_2O_2(aq) \xrightarrow{\text{catalyst}} 2H_2O(l) + O_2(g)$$

The following sentences describe a practical investigation designed to show that after catalysing the reaction, the manganese(IV) oxide is unchanged in mass. The sentences are not in the correct order. Write the letters in order to show the correct sequence of actions.

TIP

When you put an investigation in order, you must check your answer. Imagine yourself working through each step.

Correct order: ....

P	Once the reaction has finished, the mixture is filtered through the weighed filter paper.
Q	The manganese(IV) oxide is added to some hydrogen peroxide in a boiling tube. A glowing spill is used to test for oxygen given off.
R	The dried manganese(IV) oxide and filter paper are weighed.
S	The mass of the dried manganese(IV) oxide and filter paper is compared with their combined mass at the beginning.
T	The manganese(IV) oxide and filter paper are placed in an oven and left to dry.
U	Some manganese(IV) oxide is weighed out and the mass recorded.
V	All the manganese(IV) oxide is washed from the boiling tube and filtered through the weighed filter paper.
W	A filter paper is weighed and its mass recorded.

Practice

2 In this exercise, you will look at a reaction that is sped up by different substances. A catalyst speeds up a chemical reaction and is *unchanged chemically* at the end of the reaction. A false catalyst also speeds up a reaction but is *changed chemically* at the end of the reaction.

Zinc reacts with sulfuric acid to form hydrogen gas and zinc sulfate solution. The substances investigated as catalysts were copper metal (pink–brown solid) and blue copper(II) sulfate solution. The speed of the reaction was monitored by observing the bubbles of hydrogen gas formed.

The results are shown in Table 6.3.

Tube	Contents	Observations
A	zinc granule + sulfuric acid	a few bubbles
B	zinc granule + sulfuric acid + copper metal	rapid evolution of bubbles copper metal unchanged in appearance and mass after drying
C	zinc granule + sulfuric acid + few drops of copper(II) sulfate solution	rapid evolution of bubbles pink–brown solid formed

Table 6.3: Observations when zinc reacts with sulfuric acid.

a Explain which of the two substances, copper or copper(II) sulfate, is *not* a catalyst for the reaction even though it speeds up the reaction (a false catalyst).

answer ....

explanation ....

b Which of the two substances, copper or copper(II) sulfate, is a true catalyst for the reaction?

answer ....

explanation ....

....

Challenge

3 A catalyst speeds up a reaction by reducing the activation energy of the reaction.

  a On Figure 6.9:

- draw the reaction pathway for the uncatalysed reaction between zinc and sulfuric acid

- label the activation energy for this uncatalysed reaction

- label the enthalpy change for the reaction.

  b On the same diagram:

- draw the reaction pathway for the catalysed reaction

- label the activation energy for the catalysed reaction.

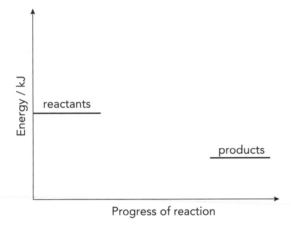

Figure 6.9: Reaction pathway diagram.

> Redox reactions

Exercise 6.6

IN THIS EXERCISE YOU WILL:

- define oxidation and reduction in terms of the addition or removal of oxygen

- identify the compound that has been oxidised or reduced in a given chemical reaction

- practise balancing symbol equations.

KEY WORDS

half-equations: ionic equations showing the reactions at the anode (oxidation) and cathode (reduction) in an electrolytic cell.

halogen displacement reactions: reactions in which a more reactive halogen displaces a less reactive halogen from a solution of its salt.

Focus

1 a Complete Figure 6.10 to show what substances are used and what is produced in burning and rusting.

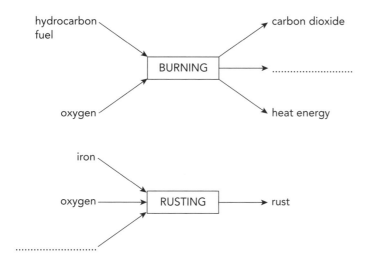

Figure 6.10: Reactions involving oxygen.

b What type of chemical change is involved in both of the reactions shown in Figure 6.10?

....

2 Oxidation and reduction reactions are important. There are several definitions of oxidation and reduction. Complete the following statements.

a If a substance gains oxygen during a reaction, it is _____ .

b If a substance _____ oxygen during a reaction, it is reduced.

KEY WORDS

oxidation: there are three definitions of oxidation:

i a reaction in which oxygen is added to an element or compound

ii a reaction involving the loss of electrons from an atom, molecule or ion

iii a reaction in which the oxidation state of an element is increased.

redox reaction: a reaction involving both reduction and oxidation.

reduction: there are three definitions of reduction:

i a reaction in which oxygen is removed from a compound

ii a reaction involving the gain of electrons by an atom, molecule or ion

iii a reaction in which the oxidation state of an element is decreased.

Practice

3 Figure 6.11 shows a: the oxidation of copper to copper(II) oxide and b: the reduction of copper(II) oxide back to copper using hydrogen.

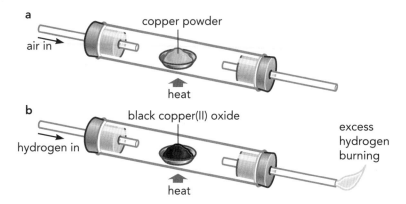

Figure 6.11: Oxidation and reduction reactions involving copper.

a Fill in the boxes in Figure 6.12 with the appropriate terms.

copper(II) oxide + hydrogen $\xrightarrow{\text{heat}}$ copper + water

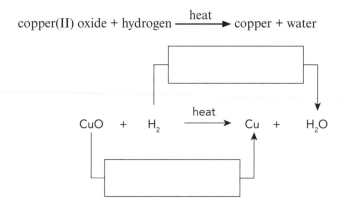

Figure 6.12: An oxidation and reduction reaction.

b Equations i–iv show unbalanced symbol equations that represent redox reactions involving metal oxides and other substances. For each reaction:

- if necessary, balance the equation
- circle the substance being reduced
- underline the substance being oxidised.

i ....Zn(s) + ...$Ag_2O(s) \rightarrow$ ....$ZnO(s)$ + ...$Ag(s)$

ii ....$Fe_2O_3(s)$ + ...$Al(s) \rightarrow$ ....$Fe(s)$ + ...$Al_2O_3(s)$

iii ....$Mg(s)$ + ...$Al_2O_3(s) \rightarrow$ ....$MgO(s)$ + ...$Al(s)$

iv ....$CO_2(g)$ + ...$Mg(s) \rightarrow$ ....$C(s)$ + ...$MgO(s)$

Challenge

4 Catalytic converters (Figure 6.13) reduce the pollution from motor vehicles by converting polluting gases in the exhaust fumes into less harmful gases.

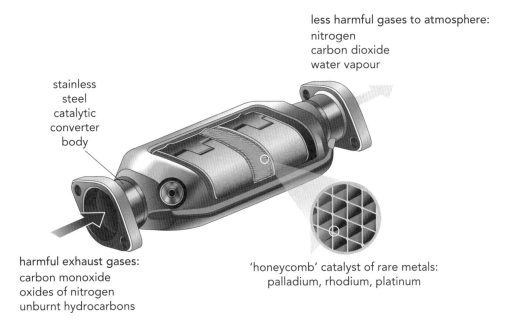

less harmful gases to atmosphere:
nitrogen
carbon dioxide
water vapour

stainless
steel
catalytic
converter
body

harmful exhaust gases:
carbon monoxide
oxides of nitrogen
unburnt hydrocarbons

'honeycomb' catalyst of rare metals:
palladium, rhodium, platinum

Figure 6.13: A catalytic converter.

Car exhaust fumes contain gases such as carbon monoxide (CO), nitrogen monoxide (nitrogen(II) oxide, NO) and unburnt hydrocarbons. The catalytic converter converts these to carbon dioxide (CO_2), nitrogen (N_2) and water (H_2O) in reactions such as those shown here (a–c).

For each reaction, explain why it is a redox reaction and identify the substances that are reduced and oxidised.

a carbon monoxide + oxygen → carbon dioxide

$CO(g)$ + $O_2(g)$ → $2CO_2(g)$

....

....

b nitrogen monoxide + carbon monoxide → nitrogen + carbon dioxide

$2NO(g)$ + $2CO(g)$ → $N_2(g)$ + $2CO_2(g)$

....

....

> **TIP**
>
> In a redox reaction, both oxidation and reduction take place at the same time. The oxidising agent brings about oxidation but is itself reduced in the process.

c   hydrocarbons + oxygen → carbon dioxide + water

One of the unburnt hydrocarbons from the fuel could be heptane.
Complete the balanced symbol equation for the reaction for heptane.
Then explain why it is a redox reaction and identify the substances
that are reduced and oxidised.

$C_7H_{16} + ...O_2 → 7............ + 8H_2O$

....

....

Exercise 6.7

IN THIS EXERCISE YOU WILL:

- extend the definitions of oxidation and reduction to reactions in which reactants lose and gain electrons

- consider the transfer of electrons from one element to another as a redox reaction

- practise using and balancing half-equations, including electrode reactions in electrolysis, and relate these to reduction and oxidation

- describe how a Roman numeral is used to show the oxidation number of an element in a compound

- develop the broadest definition of redox in terms of an increase or decrease in the oxidation number of atoms present in the reactants.

Focus

1 a   A further definition of redox reactions links oxidation and reduction to the exchange of electrons during a reaction.

Complete the following statements.

i   Oxidation is the _____ of electrons.

ii   Reduction is the _____ of electrons.

b   These two electronic configurations show the changes taking place when metals and non-metals react to form ions.

For each reaction:

- fill in the gap above the arrow

- explain why it is a redox reaction

- identify the oxidising and reducing agents.

TIP

Use the mnemonic 'OIL RIG' to remember the difference between oxidation and reduction in terms of electron transfer: Oxidation Is Loss, Reduction Is Gain.

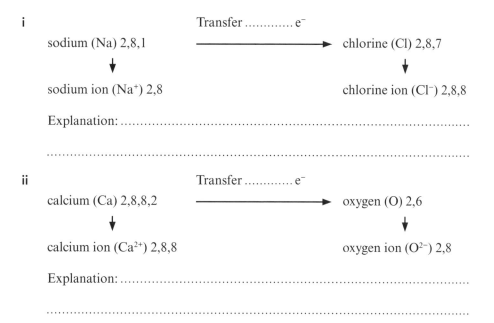

i

sodium (Na) 2,8,1 ———Transfer .... e⁻———→ chlorine (Cl) 2,8,7

sodium ion (Na⁺) 2,8   chlorine ion (Cl⁻) 2,8,8

Explanation: ....

....

ii

calcium (Ca) 2,8,8,2 ———Transfer .... e⁻———→ oxygen (O) 2,6

calcium ion (Ca²⁺) 2,8,8   oxygen ion (O²⁻) 2,8

Explanation: ....

....

Practice

2 Electrode reactions take place at the anode and the cathode during electrolysis. The half-equations a–c show reactions that take place at the anode and cathode. For each reaction:

- balance the equation
- give the electrode at which the reaction takes place
- state whether it is a reduction or oxidation reaction.

a $Cu^{2+}(aq) + ... e^- \rightarrow Cu(s)$

electrode = ...   type of reaction = ...

b $...... Cl^-(aq) \rightarrow Cl_2(g) + ... e^-$

electrode = ...   type of reaction = ...

c $Al^{3+}(l) + ... e^- \rightarrow Al(l)$

electrode = ...   type of reaction = ...

> **TIP**
>
> In an electrolytic cell, reduction always takes place at the cathode and oxidation always takes place at the anode. This is the only situation in which the processes of oxidation and reduction in an overall redox reaction are separated.

PEER ASSESSMENT

Go through Exercise 6.7 with a partner. Did you both understand the new definitions of oxidation and reduction? Can you come up with an easy memory aid?

For example: *If an atom or ion loses electrons it becomes more ... and if it gains electrons it becomes more ...*

Check your answers to see if you have understood the new way of looking at redox reactions. If you applied your memory aid, did it work?

Challenge

3 The oxidation number of an element gives us an indication of how oxidised or reduced a particular element is in a compound. What is the oxidation number of the metal in the following compounds?

    a copper(II) chloride ....

    b iron(III) oxide ....

    c iron(II) sulfate ....

    d manganese(IV) oxide ....

4 Burning magnesium will react with carbon dioxide to produce carbon.

The oxidation numbers of the elements, except oxygen, are shown beneath the formulae in the following equation.

$$2Mg(s) \quad + \quad CO_2(g) \quad \rightarrow \quad 2MgO(s) \quad + \quad C(s)$$
$$0 \qquad\qquad +4 \qquad\qquad\quad +2 \qquad\qquad 0$$

Use oxidation numbers to state which elements have been oxidised and which have been reduced in this reaction. Give the value for each change.

....

....

PEER ASSESSMENT

With your partner, look at all the exercises in this chapter.

1 If there is one exercise that you understood but your partner did not, explain to them how you understood it. Then reverse the roles so they can explain an exercise to you.

2 Look at any exercise(s) that neither of you understood. What do you need to do to improve your understanding?

Chapter 7

Acids, bases and salts

> The characteristic properties of acids and bases, and oxides

Exercise 7.1

IN THIS EXERCISE YOU WILL:

- focus on the differences between acids and alkalis in terms of the pH values of their solutions
- learn the formulae of some common laboratory acids and alkalis
- consider how the pH of a solution will tell you how acidic or how alkaline the solution is
- describe the colours of different indicators under acid, neutral and alkaline conditions
- relate the colours of universal indicator to the pH value of a solution.

Focus

1 Use the words provided to complete the following paragraph. Some words are used more than once. (*Note:* this activity continues on the next page.)

acids	alkalis	greater	hydrochloric	hydrogen

hydroxide	insoluble	less	nitric	oxides	potassium

sodium	soluble	sulfuric	water

Acids are substances that dissolve in _____ to give a solution with a pH _____ than 7. _____ acid has the formula HCl and is a strong acid. _____ acid (formula H_2SO_4) and _____ acid (formula HNO_3) are also strong _____. In acidic solutions, the concentration of _____ ions is greater than the concentration of _____ ions.

KEY WORDS

acid: a substance that dissolves in water, producing $H^+(aq)$ ions. A solution of an acid turns litmus red and has a pH below 7. Acids act as proton donors.

alkali: a soluble base that produces OH^-(aq) ions in water – a solution of an alkali turns litmus blue and has a pH above 7.

antacids: compounds used medically to treat indigestion by neutralising excess stomach acid.

base: a substance that neutralises an acid, producing a salt and water as the only products. Bases act as proton acceptors.

indicator: a substance which changes colour when added to acidic or alkaline solutions, e.g. litmus or thymolphthalein.

Bases are the _____ and hydroxides of metals and ammonia. A base

will neutralise an acid to form a salt and _____. The solutions of bases

have pH values _____ than 7. Most bases are _____ in water

but alkalis are bases that are _____ in water. KOH (_____

hydroxide) and NaOH (_____ hydroxide) are both strong _____.

In alkaline solutions, the concentration of _____ ions is greater than the

concentration of _____ ions.

Practice

2   Look at the statements in Table 7.1. Each statement describes an acid, a base or
an alkali. Put a tick (✓) in the correct column for each statement. One row of the
table has been completed as an example.

Practical observation	Acid	Base	Alkali
A solution of the substance has a pH of 8.			
A solution of the substance turns litmus paper blue.			✓
A solution of the substance turns litmus paper red.			
A substance that neutralises an acid but is insoluble in water.			
A substance that neutralises an acid and is soluble in water.			
A substance that is an insoluble oxide or hydroxide of a metal.			
A substance that is a soluble hydroxide of a metal.			
A solution with a pH of 9 that is produced when ammonia is dissolved in water.			
A solution of the substance has a pH of 3.			
A solution of the substance has a pH of 13.			

Table 7.1: Statements about acids, bases and alkalis.

KEY WORDS

litmus: the most common indicator; turns red in acid and blue in alkali.

methyl orange: an acid–base indicator that is red in acidic solutions and yellow in alkaline solutions.

pH scale: a scale running from below 0 to 14; use to express the acidity or alkalinity of a solution; a neutral solution has a pH of 7.

salts: ionic compounds made by the neutralisation of an acid with a base (or alkali), e.g. copper(II) sulfate and potassium nitrate.

thymolphthalein: an acid–base indicator that is colourless in acidic solutions and blue in alkaline solutions.

universal indicator: a mixture of indicators that has different colours in solutions of different pH.

Challenge

3   The graph in Figure 7.1 shows what happens to the pH values if sodium hydroxide solution (an alkali) is added to a solution of hydrochloric acid. At points A, B and C, samples of the mixture are removed on a glass rod and spotted onto universal indicator paper.

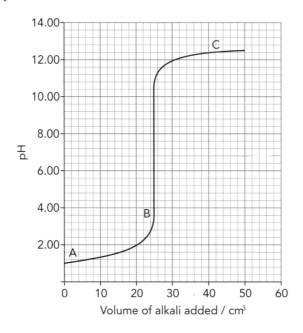

Figure 7.1: pH when different volumes of alkali are added to hydrochloric acid.

a   What is the colour of the universal indicator paper with samples A, B and C?

colour with sample A: ....

colour with sample B: ....

colour with sample C: ....

b   What would be the colour of methyl orange at pH 12? ....

c   On the graph, mark with an N where the acid is neutralised by the alkali.

d   What volume of alkali is needed to neutralise the acid? ....

e   What is the best apparatus to use to add the alkali accurately to the acid?

....

f   What is the pH of the solution when 15 cm³ of alkali have been added?

....

Exercise 7.2

IN THIS EXERCISE YOU WILL:

- reinforce your knowledge of acids
- classify oxides according to their acid–base character
- consider the reactions of acids with reactive metals, metal oxides, metal hydroxides and metal carbonates
- write the word and balanced symbol equations for these reactions
- predict the products of the reactions of acids
- interpret observations of the reactions of acids.

Focus

1   The boxes on the left describe the reactions of acids with different substances.
The boxes on the right contain statements about these reactions.

Draw lines to connect each type of reaction with the statements that are true about that reaction. You can draw more than one line from each type of reaction.

Type of reaction	Statements about these reactions
acid + metal carbonate	gives H_2 gas as a product
	gives a salt + water + a gas as the products
acid + reactive metal	gives CO_2 as a product
	produces effervescence (fizzing)
acid + insoluble metal oxide	gives a salt and water as the only products
acid + alkali	gives a salt and gas only

2   Oxides of metals and non-metals have different acid–base characteristics.
    Complete Table 7.2 to show whether the oxides of each element are acidic
    or basic.

Element	carbon	copper	phosphorus	sulfur	calcium
Acidic or basic oxide?					

Table 7.2: Acid–base characteristics of oxides.

3   a   Some metal oxides are amphoteric. Complete the following sentence to
        explain what this means.

        An amphoteric oxide ....

    b   Write balanced symbol equations to show how Al_2O_3 reacts with HCl
        and NaOH.

Practice

4   Table 7.3 gives the formulae of some different acids, bases, reactive metals, reactive
    metal carbonates and salts. Use this information to write the word and balanced
    symbol equations for reactions **a–f**.

Acid	Base/ reactive metal	Carbonate	Salt
HNO_3	NaOH	$CaCO_3$	$CaCl_2$
HCl	$Ca(OH)_2$	Na_2CO_3	NaCl
H_2SO_4	CaO		$NaNO_3$
	Mg		Na_2SO_4
			$Ca(NO_3)_2$
			$MgCl_2$

Table 7.3: Formulae of different acids, bases, reactive metal carbonates and salts.

a magnesium + hydrochloric acid

word equation:

....

symbol equation: ....

b calcium hydroxide + hydrochloric acid

word equation:

....

symbol equation: ....

c calcium oxide + nitric acid

word equation:

....

symbol equation: ....

d sodium hydroxide + sulfuric acid

word equation:

....

symbol equation: ....

e sodium carbonate + nitric acid

word equation:

....

symbol equation: ....

f magnesium + nitric acid

word equation:

....

symbol equation: ....

5 Cross out the incorrect words to complete the text. Then complete the neutralisation equation.

When an acid reacts with **water / a base**, a **neutralisation / precipitation** reaction occurs. In this reaction, the pH of the acid is **lower / higher** than that of the neutral product.

This reaction is shown by the general equation:

acid + base → _____ + _____

Challenge

6 Antacids are widely used in medicine to overcome the discomfort and problems caused by too much acid in the stomach.

A student wanted to investigate the effectiveness of two substances as antacids. The two substances to be investigated were magnesium hydroxide and magnesium carbonate.

The student was given the following apparatus and chemicals:

- two spatulas
- exactly 2g of each substance in powder form
- 250 cm³ of 0.1 mol/dm³ hydrochloric acid
- a 50 cm³ burette, conical flasks and a white tile
- access to distilled water
- methyl orange indicator.

a Give the balanced symbol equation for the reaction involving magnesium hydroxide.

....

b Give the balanced symbol equation for the reaction involving magnesium carbonate.

....

c Describe how the student could carry out their investigation using the apparatus and chemicals listed.

....

....

....

....

....

....

....

....

d If the magnesium carbonate were used as an antacid, the user might experience some additional discomfort. Explain why.

....

....

> Preparation of salts

Exercise 7.3

IN THIS EXERCISE YOU WILL:

- learn more of the characteristic reactions of acids and the types of salt produced by particular acids
- describe the method of preparing crystals of a soluble salt.

KEY WORDS

crystallisation: the process of forming crystals from a saturated solution.

filtrate: the liquid that passes through the filter paper during filtration.

limiting reactant: the reactant that is not in excess.

precipitate: an insoluble salt formed during a precipitation reaction.

Focus

Salts are produced in reactions where the hydrogen of an acid is replaced by metal ions or the ammonium ion. Each acid gives a characteristic family of salts. Sulfuric acid, for instance, always produces a sulfate.

1 Complete the following statements for other acids.

    a   Hydrochloric acid always produces a _____

    b   Nitric acid always produces a _____

    c   Phosphoric acid always produces a _____

2 Complete Table 7.4, which summarises the products of various reactions of acids.

Substances reacted together		Salt produced	Other products of the reaction
dilute hydrochloric acid	zinc oxide		
dilute sulfuric acid		copper sulfate	water, carbon dioxide
		magnesium sulfate	water, carbon dioxide
		magnesium chloride	hydrogen
dilute nitric acid	copper oxide		
dilute ethanoic acid		sodium ethanoate	water
	potassium hydroxide	potassium phosphate	

Table 7.4: Reactions that produce different types of salt.

Practice

3 Use the words provided to complete the text.

acid   anhydrous   water   combined   hydrated   hydrogen

metal   sodium   sulfuric   carbon dioxide

All salts are ionic compounds. Salts are produced when an alkali neutralises an

_____. In this reaction, the salt is formed when a _____ ion or an

ammonium ion from the alkali replaces one or more _____ ions of

the acid.

Salts can be crystallised from the solution produced by a neutralisation reaction.

The salt crystals formed often contain chemically _____ water.

These salts are called _____ salts. The salt crystals can be heated to drive

off this _____. The salt remaining is said to be _____.

Salts can be made by other reactions of acids. Magnesium sulfate can be made

by reacting magnesium carbonate with _____ acid. The gas given off is

_____. Water is also formed in this reaction.

All _____ and potassium salts are soluble in water.

Challenge

4 a State the acid and base needed to prepare magnesium sulfate.

....

b Describe briefly how magnesium sulfate is prepared.

....

....

....

....

5 Crystals of zinc sulfate can be prepared by reacting dilute sulfuric acid with excess zinc granules.

a   Why does the preparation use an excess of the metal?

....

....

b   How is the solution of zinc sulfate obtained from the reaction mixture?

....

c   Zinc sulfate is prepared by crystallisation. Describe how you would prepare pure dry crystals from zinc sulfate solution.

....

....

....

....

d   Write word and balanced symbol equations for the reaction between zinc granules and dilute sulfuric acid. Include state symbols in your symbol equation.

....

....

6 Crystals of magnesium sulfate ($MgSO_4 \cdot 7H_2O$) can be made by reacting magnesium oxide with dilute sulfuric acid.

a   The following statements describe how to prepare magnesium sulfate crystals following the reaction. The statements are not in order. Write the letters in order to show the correct sequence of actions.

A   Allow the solution to cool and crystals to form.

B   Warm the filtrate until the solution is very concentrated.

C   Pour the filtrate into an evaporating basin.

D   Wash and dry the crystals.

E   Filter the mixture to remove excess magnesium oxide.

F   Filter off the crystals.

The correct order is:

....

b   Explain why it is necessary to dry the crystals carefully at the end of the preparation rather than heating them strongly.

....

c   The formula for the compound formed is $MgSO_4 \cdot 7H_2O$. This compound contains water. What word do we use to describe compounds like this?

....

Exercise 7.4

IN THIS EXERCISE YOU WILL:

- work out combinations of reagents required to prepare an insoluble salt
- deduce the formula of an insoluble salt using a precipitation method.

Focus

1   Insoluble salts can be made using a precipitation reaction.

Figure 7.2 is a Venn diagram showing the solubility of various inorganic compounds.

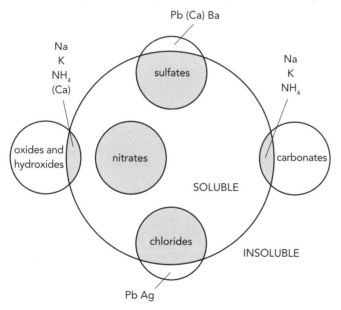

Figure 7.2: A Venn diagram showing the solubility of inorganic compounds.

Use the information in Figure 7.2 to state whether the following compounds are soluble or insoluble.

a sodium sulfate ....

b barium sulfate ....

c copper(II) hydroxide ....

d ammonium chloride ....

e lead(II) iodide ....

f sodium hydrogencarbonate. ....

Practice

2 For each of the following insoluble salts (a–d):

- give the two reagents that could be used to prepare it
- give the balanced symbol equation for the reaction taking place.

   a copper(II) carbonate

     reagents used: ....

     equation: ....

   b silver iodide

     reagents used: ....

     equation: ....

   c silver chloride

     reagents used: ....

     equation: ....

   d barium sulfate

     reagents used: ....

     equation: ....

Challenge

3 The precipitation method can be used to find the formula of a salt. In an experiment, $6\,cm^3$ of a solution of the nitrate of metal X was placed in a narrow test-tube. Then $1\,cm^3$ of aqueous sodium phosphate, Na_3PO_4, was added to the test-tube. The precipitate settled and its height was measured. The concentration of both solutions was the same.

The experiment was repeated using different volumes of the sodium phosphate solution. The results are shown on the graph in Figure 7.3.

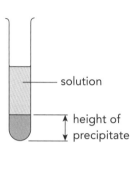
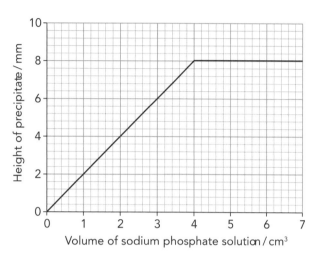

Figure 7.3: Results of a precipitation experiment.

a What is the formula of the phosphate of metal X? Give your reasoning.

....

....

....

b List the three stages by which you would obtain a dry sample of the salt following precipitation.

....

....

....

PEER ASSESSMENT

Write down the topics you found easiest and most difficult in this chapter. Share your answers with a partner. If you understood a topic that your partner did not, explain how you came to understand it.

Chapter 8
The Periodic Table

> Arrangements of elements

Exercise 8.1

IN THIS EXERCISE YOU WILL:

- consider the organisation of the Periodic Table into groups and periods
- recognise the different properties of elements in various groups and periods of the Periodic Table
- revisit the electronic basis for this arrangement
- identify periodic or repeating patterns shown by the elements
- identify trends in groups given information about the elements.

KEY WORDS

groups: vertical columns of the Periodic Table containing elements with similar chemical properties; atoms of elements in the same group have the same number of electrons in their outer energy levels.

period: a horizontal row of the Periodic Table.

periodic property: a property of the elements that shows a repeating pattern when plotted against proton number (Z).

proton number (or atomic number) (Z): the number of protons in the nucleus of an atom.

Focus

1 Use the words provided to complete the text about the Periodic Table. Not all of the words are used. Some of the words are used in both the plural and the singular form.

> column(s)　　electron(s)　　group(s)　　horizontal　　mass
>
> period(s)　　proton(s)　　row(s)　　vertical

The Periodic Table is a way of arranging the elements according to their properties. They are arranged in order of their _____ number.

Elements with similar properties are placed together in _____

_____ called _____. Periods are _____ _____ of the elements. The table shows trends down the _____ and patterns across the _____.

The placing of the elements in the table corresponds to their _____ arrangements (electronic configurations). The number of _____ in the outer _____ shell of an atom is the same as the element's _____ number in the table. The number of occupied _____ shells of the element is the _____ in which it is placed.

Practice

2 Figure 8.1 shows the upper part of the Periodic Table with certain elements named.

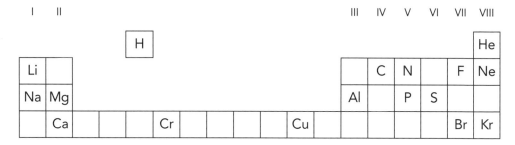

Figure 8.1: A section of the Periodic Table.

Using the elements shown in Figure 8.1, write down the symbols of the elements that answer the following questions.

a Which two elements are transition metals? ....

b Which element has just two electrons in the full outer shell of its atom?

....

c Which element is a red–brown liquid at room temperature and pressure?

....

d Which element has four electrons in the outer energy level of its atom?

....

e Which element is a yellow solid at room temperature? ....

f Which elements are noble gases? ....

g Which element has compounds that produce blue solutions when they

dissolve? ....

h Which element has the electron arrangement 2,8,8,2?

....

i Which element burns with a brilliant white flame when ignited?

....

Challenge

3 One physical property that shows a repeating pattern when plotted against proton number is the melting point of an element. Figure 8.2 shows the melting points of the elements in Periods 2 and 3 plotted against the proton number of the element.

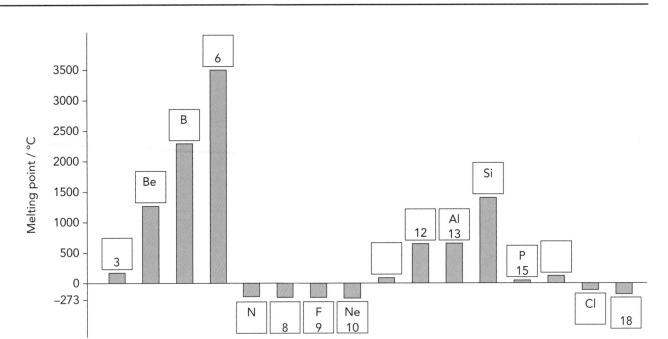

Figure 8.2: The melting points of elements in the second and third periods.

a   Complete Figure 8.2 by adding the missing element symbols and proton numbers. (There are seven missing symbols and seven missing proton numbers.)

b   From Figure 8.2, which *two* elements show the highest melting points?

.... and ....

c   To which group do these two elements belong? ....

d   Complete the following sentences describing this property of the elements.

When the melting points of elements are plotted against ....

....................................., they show a repeating ....

Elements in Group .... have the highest melting points,

while the .... gases have the lowest melting points.

4   Table 8.1 contains information about the melting point and hardness of four elements.

a   Use the information you are given to complete Table 8.1.

Element	Melting point / K	Hardness / Mohs
carbon	3500	10
silicon		6.5
germanium	937	
tin	232	1.5

Table 8.1: Properties of Group IV elements.

b   Describe the trend in melting point and hardness as we descend Group IV.

....

....

› Group I properties
Exercise 8.2

IN THIS EXERCISE YOU WILL:

- identify certain key properties of the alkali metals and how these properties change as we descend the group

- predict properties of elements from an understanding of the trends within groups or periods of the table.

KEY WORDS

alkali metals: elements in Group I of the Periodic Table; they are the most reactive group of metals.

electrical conductor: a substance that conducts electricity but is not chemically changed in the process.

insulator: a substance that does not conduct electricity.

thermal conductivity: the ability to conduct heat.

Focus

1 **a**   Circle the *one* symbol that represents the most reactive alkali metal.

         C   Ca   Cr   Cs   Cu

    b   Circle the *one* symbol for the element which has the electron arrangement 2,8,1.

         Cs   K   Li   Na   Rb

    c   Look at the electronic configuration of the element in b. Explain how you can tell that this element is in Group I of the Periodic Table.

....

....

    d   Why do elements in the same group show similar chemical properties?

....

....

    e   Circle the words that can be used to describe a Group I element.

         conductor   dense   dull   hard   inert

             insulator   lustrous   reactive   soft

Practice

2 Why are the alkali metals stored under oil?

....

....

3 A teacher demonstrated the reactions of sodium and potassium with water. The students were asked to write down their observations.

a Give *two* similar observations about the reactions of the two metals.

....

....

b Give *one* difference between the reactions of the two metals.

....

c Balance the following symbol equation for the reaction of sodium with water.

____$Na(s)$ + ____$H_2O(l)$ → ____$NaOH(aq)$ + ____$H_2(g)$

Challenge

Caesium is an alkali metal. It is in Group I of the Periodic Table.

4 a State *two* physical properties of caesium.

....

....

b State the number of electrons in the outer shell of a caesium atom.

....

5 Complete Table 8.2 to estimate the boiling point and atomic radius of caesium.

Comment also on the reactivity of potassium and caesium with water.

(*Note:* atomic radius is a measure of the size of an atom.)

Group I metal	Density/g/cm³	Radius of metal atom/nm	Boiling point/°C	Reactivity with water
sodium	0.97	0.191	883	floats and fizzes quickly on the surface; disappears gradually; does not burst into flame
potassium	0.86	0.235	760	
rubidium	1.53	0.250	686	reacts instantaneously; fizzes and bursts into flame; spits violently and may explode
caesium	1.88			

Table 8.2: Data on the alkali metals.

SELF ASSESSMENT

How confident were you at estimating the unknown values needed to complete Tables 8.1 and 8.2?

Compare your estimates with a partner and discuss the method you used to estimate values for unfamiliar data. Can you work together to come up with a strategy you could apply to various types of data?

〉 Group VII properties

Exercise 8.3

IN THIS EXERCISE YOU WILL:

- learn certain key properties of the halogen non-metals and how these properties change as we descend the group

- predict properties of elements from trends within groups or periods

- plot and interpret a graph of data for the halogens

- describe and explain displacement reactions of the halogens.

KEY WORD

halogens: elements in Group VII of the Periodic Table; generally the most reactive group of non-metals.

Focus

1 The halogens are one group of elements in the Periodic Table. Cross out the incorrect words to complete the following statements about the halogens.

   a The halogens are **metals / non-metals** and their vapours are **coloured / colourless**.

   b The halogens are **toxic / non-toxic** to humans.

   c Halogen molecules are each made of **one / two** atoms; they are **monatomic / diatomic**.

   d Halogens react with **metal / non-metal** elements to form crystalline compounds that are salts.

   e Halogens can **colour / bleach** vegetable dyes and kill bacteria.

Practice

2 a Halogens undergo displacement reactions. Complete Table 8.3 to show whether you would expect a reaction between each pair of substances.

	Chlorine	Bromine	Iodine
Chloride	X		no reaction
Bromide		X	
Iodide	displacement reaction		X

Table 8.3: Reactions between halogens.

   b For each combination in Table 8.3 that will show displacement, write a word and symbol equation to show the reaction.

   ....

   ....

   ....

   ....

   ....

   ....

Challenge

3 The elements in Group VII are known as the halogens. The properties of the halogens show distinct trends as you descend the group. Table 8.4 shows some of the physical properties of the Group VII elements at atmospheric pressure.

a   Complete Table 8.4 by filling in the spaces. You will estimate the boiling point
of bromine in part c.

Element	Proton number	Melting point / °C	Boiling point / °C	Colour
fluorine	9	−219	−188	pale yellow
chlorine	17	−101	−34	pale green
bromine	35	−6		
iodine	53	114	185	grey–black
astatine	85	303	337	

Table 8.4: Some properties of the halogens.

b   On the grid provided, plot a graph of the melting points and boiling points
of the halogens against their proton numbers. Join the points for each
property to produce two separate lines on the graph.

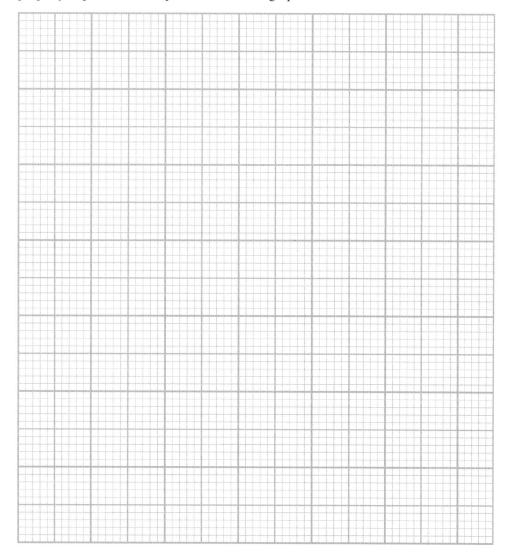

c Draw a line across the graph at 20 °C to help you decide which elements are solid, liquid or gas at room temperature and pressure.

d Use your graph to estimate the boiling point of bromine. State its colour and physical state at room temperature.

estimated boiling point: .... °C

colour: ....

physical state: ....

e State which of the halogens are gases at room temperature and pressure.

....

f Astatine is very rarely seen. Predict its physical state and colour at room temperature and pressure.

....

g Describe the trend in the melting points of the halogens as you go down the group.

....

> ## TIP

The trends in chemical reactivity run in opposite directions in metallic and non-metallic groups of the Periodic Table. For metallic groups, reactivity increases down the group. For non-metallic groups, reactivity decreases down the group.

> Transition elements and the noble gases

Exercise 8.4

IN THIS EXERCISE YOU WILL:

- review the properties of the transition elements
- distinguish between transition and non-transition elements
- assign properties to the appropriate transition element
- consider the meanings of the Roman numerals used in the naming of transition element compounds
- revisit electronic configurations and use them to identify elements
- interpret data on the properties of the noble gases.

KEY WORDS

noble gases: elements in Group VIII; a group of stable, very unreactive gases.

transition metals (transition elements): elements from the central region of the Periodic Table; they are hard, strong, dense metals that form compounds that are often coloured.

Focus

1 Table 8.5 contains statements about the transition elements. Tick (✓) the appropriate boxes to show whether each statement is true or false.

	True	False
Some transition elements are non-metals.		
Transition elements have high densities.		
Some transition elements make good catalysts.		
Transition elements form only white compounds.		
All transition elements are magnetic.		

Table 8.5: The physical properties of the transition elements.

Practice

2 Read the following statements about metals. For each statement, name the transition element that can be used as described, or that fits the description. (*Note:* you may need to use the internet to find out the answers.)

a Used for water pipes: ....

b Part of the catalyst used in car exhausts: ....

c Forms a blue sulfate compound: ....

d A magnetic element: ....

e The transition element in the compound $KMnO_4$: ....

f Can be used to plate car bumpers: ....

g Can be used in jewellery: ....

Challenge

3 The noble gases (Group VIII) are unreactive, monatomic gases. Table 8.6 shows data for some of the noble gases.

Noble gas	Density / g / dm³	Atomic number	Period	Electronic configuration
helium	0.18	2	1	
neon	0.90	10	2	2,8
argon	1.78	18		2,8, ——
krypton	3.75	36		2,8,18,8
xenon	5.89	54	5	2,8,18,18,8

Table 8.6: Data on some of the noble gases.

(*Note:* the density of air is 1.28 g/dm³.)

a Complete the missing period numbers and electronic configurations in Table 8.6.

b What is the relationship between the period an element is in and the number of occupied shells (energy levels) in an atom of that element?

....

c Explain why helium gas is used to fill balloons.

....

....

d If a balloon was filled with argon, would it fall to the ground or rise into the air? Explain your answer.

....

....

> TIP
>
> The stability of the noble gas configuration of electrons is very important in understanding both ionic and covalent chemical bonding. During reactions, most atoms form bonds to achieve the electronic configuration of their nearest noble gas.

> Chapter 9
Metals

> Properties and uses of metals

Exercise 9.1

IN THIS EXERCISE YOU WILL:

- investigate the general physical properties of metals and non-metals
- show how the chemical and physical properties of metals support the ways in which they are used.

KEY WORDS

malleable: a word used to describe a metal that can be bent and beaten into sheets.

sonorous: a word used to describe a metallic substance that rings like a bell when hit with a hammer.

Focus

Metals have several physical properties in common. Most metals show these properties. This is why metals are so useful.

1   Table 9.1 describes some physical properties of metals. Use the words or phrases provided to complete the first two columns. Then identify a use for metals based on each property.

high density   **electrical conductivity**   **malleability**

strength   **transfer heat well**   **require a lot of energy to melt**

Description of physical property	Name for this property	Use that depends on this property
can be moulded or bent into shape		
	thermal conductivity	
conduct electricity		
heavy for their volume		
can bear weight and do not break easily		
	high melting point	

Table 9.1: The properties and uses of metals.

Practice

2   The physical properties of non-metals tend to differ from those of metals.
    Complete the following sentences by stating the general property of non-metals in
    each case.

a   Metals show good electrical conductivity whereas non-metals are ....

    ....

b   Metals are malleable but non-metals are ....

    ....

c   Metals are good conductors of heat but most non-metals are ....

    ....

d   Metals are usually solids while non-metals are ....

    ....

Challenge

3   Table 9.2 shows some properties of a selection of pure metals.

Metal	Relative abundance in Earth's crust	Cost of extraction	Density	Strength	Melting point / °C	Electrical conductivity relative to iron
iron	2nd	low	high	high	1535	1.0
titanium	7th	very high	low	high	1660	0.2
aluminium	1st	high	low	medium	660	3.5
zinc	19th	low	high	low	419	1.7
copper	20th	low	high	medium	1083	6.0
tin	40th	low	high	low	231	0.9
lead	30th	low	very high	low	327	0.5

Table 9.2: The properties of certain metals.

Use information from Table 9.2 to answer the following questions.

a   Why is aluminium used for overhead power cables?

    ....

b   Aluminium has low density. Why is this an advantage when aluminium is used for overhead power cables?

....

c   Why is copper used in home electrical wiring, instead of aluminium?

....

d   Why is titanium a good metal to use for jet aircraft and Formula 1 racing cars?

....

....

〉 Alloys and their properties
Exercise 9.2

IN THIS EXERCISE YOU WILL:

- investigate the nature of alloys and explore how the properties of alloys are linked to their uses

- explain how different-sized atoms in the structure of an alloy make the alloy stronger or harder than the pure metals.

KEY WORDS

alloys: mixtures of elements (usually metals) designed to have properties that are useful for a particular purpose; e.g. solder is an alloy of tin and lead, with a low melting point.

brass: an alloy of copper and zinc; this alloy is hard.

stainless steel: an alloy of iron that resists corrosion; this alloy contains a significant proportion of chromium so it is resistant to rusting.

Focus

1 Metals and their alloys play a big part in our everyday lives. Some metals are very familiar to us. Draw lines to link the properties on the left with the metals on the right.

Properties of metals

an alloy that looks like gold	
a metal that is liquid at room temperature	
an alloy of iron that does not rust	
a metal with a low density that resists corrosion	
a very unreactive precious metal	
a metal with good electrical conductivity used in wiring	

Metals

gold

aluminium

brass

copper

stainless steel

mercury

Practice

2 a Table 9.3 describes the composition and usefulness of some alloys.
Complete Table 9.3 by filling in the gaps.

Alloy	Composition	Use	Useful property
stainless steel	iron: 74% ....: 18% nickel: 8%	................, surgical instruments, ...	resistant to corrosion (does not rust easily)
brass	copper: 70% ....: 30%	.... instruments, ornaments	'gold' colour, harder than copper

Table 9.3: The composition and usefulness of two alloys.

b Draw a diagram to show the structure of an alloy.

c Use your diagram to explain the difference between the structure of a pure metal and that of an alloy.

....

....

....

....

Challenge

3 Alloys have different properties to the metals from which they are made. They are usually harder and stronger, more resistant to corrosion and have lower melting points.

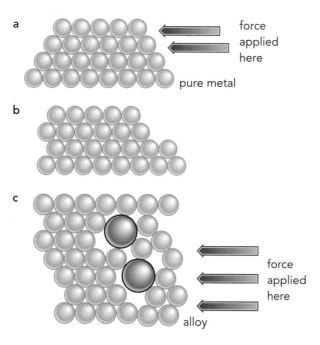

Figure 9.1: a: and **b:** The effects of applying a force to a pure metal. **c:** The effects of applying a force to an alloy.

a   Use information from Figure 9.1a and b to explain why metals are malleable (why they change shape when a force is applied).

   ....

   ....

b   Stainless steel is a form of steel. It is made by alloying iron with two other metals to make it resistant to corrosion (rusting). State which block of the Periodic Table these two other metals come from.

   ....

c   Figure 9.1c represents the structure of an alloy of the metal. Explain how the alloy is stronger than the metals from which it is made.

   ....

d   Commercial aluminium used in construction and engineering is 99.5% pure. This aluminium contains some iron and silicon. Explain why industries prefer to use this form of aluminium, rather than pure aluminium.

   ....

   ....

e   Brass is an alloy of copper and zinc. There are two main types of brass: 60:40 and 70:30 copper to zinc. The larger the proportion of zinc, the harder and stronger the alloy.

   Brass is used to make brass musical instruments and to make electrical connectors and plugs. Suggest and explain which alloy is used for each of these purposes.

   i   Cu 60:Zn 40

      ....

      ....

   ii   Cu 70:Zn 30

      ....

      ....

> TIP
>
> The ability to draw detailed diagrams of metallic bonding and the layered structure of pure metals and alloys is important. It will help you to explain the electrical conductivity of metals and the strength of alloys.

> Reactivity series

Exercise 9.3

IN THIS EXERCISE YOU WILL:

- consider how the reactivity of metals changes within a group of the Periodic Table
- investigate how the reactions of metals with water and steam show which metals are more reactive than others.

Focus

In the Periodic Table, elements are arranged in vertical columns known as groups. Each group contains elements with similar chemical properties. Within a group, there are trends in both chemical reactivity and physical properties.

1   The elements sodium and potassium are in Group I (the alkali metals) of the Periodic Table. When they are added to cold water, there is a strong reaction in both cases. If a few drops of indicator solution are added to the water, the colour change shows that the water is alkaline.

   a   Explain why these metals are part of a group called the alkali metals.

   ....

   ....

   b   Give the electronic configurations of sodium and potassium.

   sodium: ....

   potassium: ....

   c   What feature of the electronic configurations of sodium and potassium places them in Group I of the Periodic Table?

   ....

   d   When sodium is added to water, it melts and skids over the surface. It also fizzes as hydrogen gas is given off. Potassium reacts with water with a burst of energy which causes the hydrogen to burn with a purple flame. Explain which of these metals is more reactive when added to cold water.

   ....

   e   Write a word equation for the reaction of potassium with water.

   ....

KEY WORDS

displacement reaction: a reaction in which a more reactive element displaces a less reactive element from a solution of its salt.

reactivity series of metals: an order of reactivity, giving the most reactive metal first, based on results from a range of experiments involving metals reacting with oxygen, water, dilute hydrochloric acid and metal salt solutions.

f Complete the balanced symbol equation for the reaction between potassium and water.

........K(s) + ...(l) → 2KOH(aq) + ... (g)

Practice

2 A student carried out some experiments to investigate the reactivity of some common metals.

First, they placed pieces of four different metals into test-tubes of dilute hydrochloric acid.

Figure 9.2 shows the progress of the reactions after a few minutes.

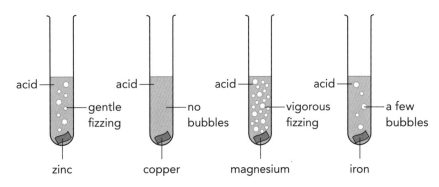

Figure 9.2: The progress of the reactions of four metals with acid.

a Use the information in Figure 9.2 to put the metals in order of decreasing reactivity.

....

b Explain why you have put the metals in this order.

....

c Name the gas being given off in all the reactions.

....

d Write the word equation for the reaction between zinc and hydrochloric acid.

....

3 The student was given further samples of three metals, labelled A, B and C. Each metal was put into cold water to see if there was any reaction. If no reaction occurred, the sample was tested to see if it reacted with steam. The results are shown in Table 9.4.

Metal sample	Reaction with cold water	Reaction with steam
A	no reaction	no reaction
B	reacted very vigorously; hydrogen gas produced	
C	no reaction	reacted strongly; metal coated with white solid; hydrogen gas produced

Table 9.4: The reactions of three metals with water and steam.

a Metal C was magnesium. Name the white solid produced in the reaction with steam.

....

b One of the other metals was sodium. Suggest whether sodium was metal A or metal B. Name the solution that remained after the reaction was complete in this case.

....

c Write the three metals in order of increasing reactivity.

....

d State which of these metals must be kept under oil to prevent it from reacting with oxygen in the air.

....

e Metal C burns in air to produce a white compound. State the name and formula of this compound.

....

SELF ASSESSMENT

You should be able to review a series of experiments involving different metals and use the results to predict an order of reactivity. How confident did you feel when answering the questions here and listing the metals in order? Are you familiar with the language and terms used?

Challenge

4   Magnesium, calcium, strontium and barium are metals in Group II of the Periodic Table. Table 9.5 describes some properties of these metals. The atomic radius of a metal atom is a measure of the size of that atom.

a   State the number of electrons in the outer shell of an atom of any of these metals.

....

b   Complete Table 9.5 by commenting on the reactivity of strontium with water and steam.

Group II metal	Density / g/ cm³	Atomic radius / nm	Boiling point / °C	Reactivity with water and steam
magnesium	1.74	0.173	1090	reacts very slowly with cold water; reacts strongly with steam
calcium	1.54	0.231	1484	reacts strongly with cold water; unsafe to react with steam
strontium	2.64	0.249	1377	
barium	3.62	0.268	1845	reacts strongly with cold water; unsafe to react with steam

Table 9.5: Properties of some Group II metals.

c   What trend do you see in atomic size as you descend Group II?

....

d   Consider the values for the density and boiling point of these metals. Suggest which metal shows values that do not fit the general trend as you descend the group.

....

e   Write the word and balanced symbol equations for the reaction of calcium with water. Include state symbols in the symbol equation.

....

....

f   State the trend in reactivity with water and steam that is seen when descending a group of metals.

....

TIP
Remember: metals that react with cold water produce the metal hydroxide as a product. Metals that only react with steam produce the metal oxide.

Exercise 9.4

IN THIS EXERCISE YOU WILL:

- describe how the reactivity of metals changes within a group of the Periodic Table
- show how the results from experiments contribute to the organisation of the reactivity series
- describe how the ability of metals to form positive ions relates to a series of metal displacement reactions.

Focus

1   Use the words provided to complete the text about the reactivity of metals.

acids   alkaline   cold   hydrogen

lower   oxide   red   steam

When metals react with _____ water, the products are a metal hydroxide

and _____. The hydroxides formed are _____ and they will turn

_____ litmus blue.

Some metals do not react with cold water but do react with _____.

The products in these reactions are the metal _____ and hydrogen.

Copper does not react with water or with dilute _____. This is because it

is _____ in the reactivity series than hydrogen.

The results of various different types of chemical reaction can be used to arrange the metals into the reactivity series.

2   **a**   Zinc does not react with cold water but it does react with steam to give zinc oxide and a gas. Write the word equation for the reaction between zinc and steam.

....

   b   Choose *one* metal from the reactivity series that will not react with steam.

....

   c   Choose *one* metal (other than zinc) from the reactivity series that will safely react with dilute sulfuric acid.

....

Practice

3 When a metal is added to a solution of the salt of a less reactive metal, a displacement reaction takes place. The equations for two different displacement reactions are:

$$Fe(s) + CuSO_4(aq) \rightarrow Cu(s) + FeSO_4(aq)$$

zinc + copper sulfate → copper + zinc sulfate

A student measures the energy change involved in these reactions by using this method:

- Place 50 cm³ of 0.5 mol/dm³ copper(II) sulfate solution in a polystyrene cup. Measure and record the temperature of the solution.

- Add 5 g of metal powder to the copper(II) sulfate solution. Stir the reaction mixture continuously and measure the temperature every 30 seconds for three minutes.

The student's data are shown in Table 9.6.

Time/minutes		0.0	0.5	1.0	1.5	2.0	2.5	3.0
Temperature/°C	Experiment 1 (zinc)	21	48	62	71	75	72	70
	Experiment 2 (iron)	21	25	32	38	41	43	44

Table 9.6: Data on the thermochemistry of metal displacement reactions.

a Plot *two* graphs on the grid provided. Plot, on one set of axes, two lines, one for each metal. Label each graph with the name of the metal.

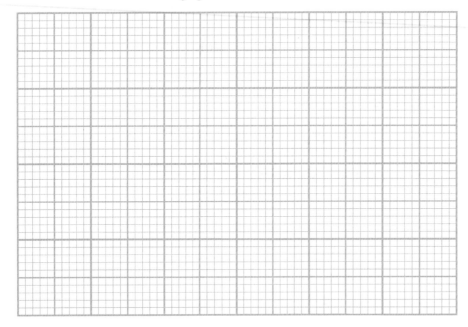

TIP

When you draw a graph, ensure the scales for the axes use more than half of the graph grid in both directions. Choose appropriate scales; for example, use 2 cm on the graph grid to represent 10, 20 or 50 units of the variable. (*Note:* the axis scales do not necessarily have to begin at zero.)

SELF ASSESSMENT

You must draw graphs accurately so the experimental results can be clearly interpreted. Look at your graph. Have you chosen a suitable scale for each axis so you can plot the values easily? Have you drawn suitable lines of best fit using the points plotted?

How did your background knowledge of displacement reactions help you to choose the best lines to draw for zinc and iron?

b Use your graphs to comment on which reaction gave the steepest initial increase in temperature.

....

c Why does the temperature stop rising for the reaction in Experiment 1 after 2 minutes?

....

d Write the balanced symbol equation for the reaction in Experiment 1.

....

e Write the word equation for the reaction in Experiment 2.

....

f State which metal, iron or zinc, produced the larger temperature rise. Suggest why this metal gave the larger temperature rise.

....

....

g Comment on whether this experiment is a 'fair test', giving a good indication as to which metal is more reactive (zinc or iron). Explain your answer.

....

....

....

....

TIP

When carrying out an experiment that is a 'fair test' you should make sure that everything is the same except the thing you are testing. Only the independent variable (e.g. time) has been allowed to affect the dependent variable.

Challenge

4   In each of the experiments shown in Table 9.7, a piece of metal is placed in a solution of a metal salt.

   a   Complete the table of observations.

		zinc tin(II) chloride solution	zinc copper(II) sulfate solution	tin copper(II) sulfate solution	silver copper(II) sulfate solution	copper silver nitrate solution
At start	Colour of metal	grey		silver coloured	silver coloured	
	Colour of solution	colourless		blue	blue	colourless
At finish	Colour of metal	coated with silver-coloured crystals		coated with brown solid	silver coloured	coated with silver-coloured crystals
	Colour of solution	colourless		colourless	blue	

Table 9.7: The results of several metal displacement reactions.

   b   Use these results to place the metals copper, silver, tin and zinc in order of reactivity. Put the most reactive metal first.

   _____ > _____ > _____ > _____

5   The reactivity of metals is directly related to the ease with which they form positive ions. The electrons lost from the metal atoms are those in the outer energy level (the valency electrons). The ease of loss of the valency electrons depends on:

   • how far the outer shell is from the nucleus of the atom

   • the number of inner shells of electrons there are

   • the number of protons in the nucleus.

   Considering these factors, explain why:

   a   magnesium is less reactive than sodium, even though its outer electrons are in the same energy level

   ....

   ....

   ....

TIP

Question 4 asks you to apply your knowledge of certain metals to other metals you are unfamiliar with. You should be prepared to do this: do not be put off by such questions. The ability to apply your knowledge of principles and concepts to a new situation is an important part of learning.

b   potassium is more reactive than sodium.

....

....

....

› Corrosion of metals

Exercise 9.5

IN THIS EXERCISE YOU WILL:

- investigate the factors involved in the rusting of iron
- consider some of the different methods used to prevent rusting.

KEY WORD

rusting: the corrosion of iron and steel to form rust (hydrated iron(III) oxide).

Focus

1   Figure 9.3 shows the results of an experiment to investigate the conditions needed for iron to rust.

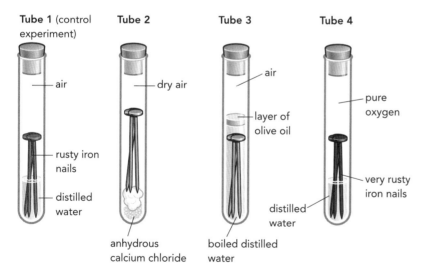

Figure 9.3: Results of an experiment on the rusting of iron.

a   What is the purpose of the anhydrous calcium chloride in the second tube?

....

b   Why is boiled distilled water used in tube 3?

....

c   What is the purpose of the oil layer in tube 3?

....

d   In which tube does the iron rust most?

....

e   What could have been added to the water to make the nails rust even more
than they did in this tube?

....

2   **a**   In addition to the iron or steel object, what *two* substances need to be present
for rusting to occur?

....

b   Barrier methods can be used to prevent rusting. Give *two* examples of barrier
methods that exclude the substances mentioned in part a.

....

....

Practice

3   Food cans (see Figure 9.4) are usually made from steel. Steel can corrode,
which limits the length of time for which food can be stored.

Figure 9.4: A typical food can.

The outside of a food can may be coated with a substance that acts as a barrier
to air and water. The inside presents more of a problem. Many of the substances
which could be used may be toxic if they combine with the food inside the can.

Air and water cannot reach the food inside the can. However, many types of food contain acids which can attack the steel of the can. One solution is to coat the steel can with another metal. Some possible metals (together with iron) are listed in order of reactivity:

(most reactive) aluminium > zinc > iron > tin > lead (least reactive)

a Why might rust on the outside of the can affect the food?

....

....

b Why would zinc be a good metal for the outside of the can?

....

....

c Why would zinc be a bad choice for the inside of the can?

....

....

d Why would tin be a good choice for the inside of the can?

....

....

Challenge

4 Tin is now used to coat both the inside and outside of food cans.

a The first cans used lead but this is no longer used even though lead is less reactive than tin. Suggest why.

....

....

b If a food can is damaged or dented, it may corrode rapidly. Suggest why damaging the layer of tin might cause this to happen.

....

....

5 Coating an iron or steel object with zinc is a useful barrier method to prevent rusting.

    a What name is given to coating an object with zinc?

    ....

    b Coating with zinc prevents rusting even if the protective layer is scratched or broken. Why does this happen?

    ....

    ....

6 It is possible to protect against rusting using blocks of a metal that is more reactive than iron. This is known as sacrificial protection. Figure 9.5 shows zinc blocks attached to the hull of a yacht to prevent rusting.

Figure 9.5: A large motor yacht in dry dock showing propellers and zinc blocks attached to the hull.

Sacrificial protection uses blocks of a metal that is higher in the reactivity series than iron. Such metals react to form cations more readily than iron.

    a Name another metal that is often used for sacrificial protection.

    ....

    b Complete the following half-equation showing the formation of zinc ions during sacrificial protection.

      $Zn(\underline{\quad}) \rightarrow Zn^{2+}(\underline{\quad}) + \underline{\quad}e^-$

> **TIP**
>
> When answering question 6a, think carefully about the conditions the blocks will be under. This will help you to identify an appropriate metal to use.

› Extraction of metals

Exercise 9.6

IN THIS EXERCISE YOU WILL:
• describe how reactivity affects the way in which metals are extracted
• investigate how reduction can be used in the extraction of metals.

KEY WORDS

blast furnace: a furnace for extracting metals (particularly iron) by reduction with carbon; a blast furnace uses hot air blasted in at the base of the furnace to raise the temperature.

Focus

1 Table 9.8 shows the order of reactivity of some metals in the reactivity series. The position of carbon is also shown.

Metal	Reactivity	Method of extraction	Energy needed to extract the metal	Cost of extracting the metal
sodium				
calcium				
magnesium				
aluminium				
carbon				
zinc				
lead				
copper				
silver				
gold				

Table 9.8: The reactivity of metals and their extraction.

a Draw an arrow in the second column of the table to show the increasing reactivity of the metals.

b Label the third column in the table with either 'reduction by heating with carbon' or 'extraction by electrolysis' in the appropriate spaces.

c Draw an arrow in the fourth column to show the trend in the energy required to extract the metal, from 'most' to 'least'.

d Draw an arrow in the fifth column to show the trend in the cost of extraction, from 'highest' to 'lowest'.

Practice

2 Which is the most reactive metal that can be extracted from its oxide by using carbon?

....

3 Could hydrogen be used to extract this metal from its ore? Explain your answer.

....

....

4 The main ore of sodium is rock salt (sodium chloride). State how sodium can be obtained from this ore.

....

....

> ### KEY WORDS
>
> **limestone:** a form of calcium carbonate ($CaCO_3$).
>
> **ore:** a naturally occurring mineral from which a metal can be extracted.
>
> **slag:** a molten mixture of impurities, mainly calcium silicate, formed in a blast furnace.

Challenge

5 Aluminium is extracted by electrolysis. This requires energy to work.

a What name is given to reactions that take in energy?

....

b Define the process of electrolysis.

....

....

Exercise 9.7

IN THIS EXERCISE YOU WILL:

- show how the blast furnace can be used to extract iron and other metals from their ores

- describe the details of the blast furnace process for the extraction of iron.

Focus

Iron and zinc are both extracted from their oxides using a blast furnace.

1   Figure 9.6 shows a diagram of the blast furnace for extracting iron. A, B, C, D and E show where various important substances enter or leave the furnace.

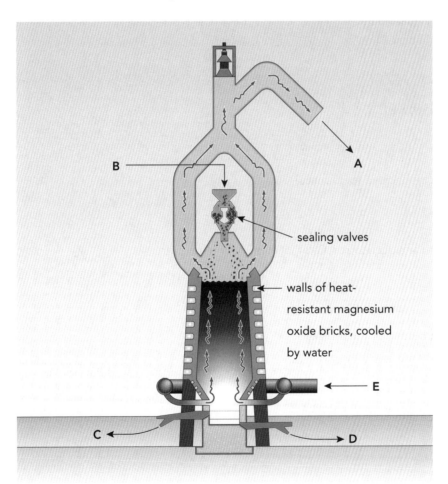

sealing valves

walls of heat-resistant magnesium oxide bricks, cooled by water

Figure 9.6: The blast furnace for extraction of iron.

Write a letter, A to E, to identify where:

a   hot air enters the furnace: ....

b   molten slag leaves the furnace: ....

c   waste gases leave the furnace to be recycled: ....

d   iron ore, coke and limestone are fed into the furnace: ....

e   molten iron leaves the furnace: ....

2   Why is the furnace used to extract iron called a blast furnace?

....

Practice

3   In the blast furnace, iron is extracted from its ore.

a   What is the name of the main ore of iron?

....

b   Where in the furnace is iron reduced?

....

c   What gas is the actual reducing agent in the furnace?

....

d   Write the word equation for the reduction reaction that converts iron ore into iron in the furnace.

....

e   Why does iron collect at the bottom of the furnace?

....

Challenge

4 Write the balanced symbol equation, including state symbols, for:

    a the reduction reaction converting iron ore into iron in the furnace

    ....

    ....

    b the thermal decomposition of limestone to lime.

    ....

    ....

5 Slag (calcium silicate) is a salt produced by a neutralisation reaction. Identify the acid and base which react.

    a The acid is ....

    b The base is ....

    c Write the balanced symbol equation for this reaction between acidic and basic oxides.

    ....

6 Zinc can also be extracted from zinc oxide by carbon reduction in a blast furnace.

    a Zinc boils at 907 °C. State why zinc is collected as a liquid at the top of the furnace.

    ....

    ....

    ....

    b The liquid iron collected at the bottom of the furnace is impure. State why the liquid zinc condensed at the top of the furnace is pure, but the liquid iron at the bottom of the furnace is impure.

    ....

    ....

    ....

> **TIP**
>
> The addition of limestone to the furnace is quite specific to the extraction of iron. Its role in providing calcium oxide to react with the silica that contaminates the iron ore is vital. Otherwise, glass would form in the furnace from the heated silica and this would stop the furnace working.

Chapter 10

Chemistry of the environment

> Air quality and climate

Exercise 10.1

IN THIS EXERCISE YOU WILL:

- identify the names and formulae of gases found in the atmosphere

- describe the composition of clean dry air

- identify which atmospheric gases are pollutants and investigate the sources of these pollutants

- consider the problems caused by different air pollutants and the methods of reducing the levels of these pollutants

- explain how we can reduce the negative effects of pollution.

KEY WORDS

acid rain: rain that has been made more acidic than normal by the presence of dissolved pollutants such as sulfur dioxide (SO_2) and oxides of nitrogen (nitrogen oxides, NO_x).

atmosphere: the layer of air and water vapour surrounding the Earth.

catalytic converter: a device for converting polluting exhaust gases from cars into less dangerous emissions.

clean dry air: air containing no water vapour and only the gases which are always present in the air.

climate change: changes in weather patterns brought about by global warming.

Focus

1 Table 10.1 gives the formulae of ten gases.

a Find the names of eight of these gases in Figure 10.1. Names of gases may be written in any direction, including diagonally.

Write the name of each gas in the correct row of Table 10.1.

A	R	G	L	A	N	S	H	I	F	O	M	T	I	L	E
M	C	H	O	R	I	C	P	R	E	U	M	A	S	D	B
O	U	T	T	I	C	R	H	N	O	Y	L	O	I	S	F
T	H	I	S	U	L	F	U	R	D	I	O	X	I	D	E
A	L	B	O	R	I	T	A	S	K	R	O	Y	Z	P	L
S	V	R	M	J	P	H	G	T	I	N	T	G	A	Q	U
Q	K	L	C	F	E	G	S	E	O	N	L	E	C	D	P
N	R	E	N	A	H	T	E	M	S	O	U	N	P	Y	F
H	Y	D	R	O	G	E	N	L	E	G	N	P	Z	L	R
B	E	N	X	R	U	O	P	A	V	R	E	T	A	W	A
W	R	O	M	I	B	A	R	T	S	A	O	T	F	A	M
F	N	P	Q	R	V	P	E	S	L	P	R	M	N	E	D
F	R	K	A	E	A	L	M	S	P	V	Y	L	P	A	O
P	S	C	A	R	B	O	N	D	I	O	X	I	D	E	M

Figure 10.1: Gases wordsearch puzzle.

Formula	Name of gas	Found in clean dry air	Considered a pollutant
Ar			
CO_2			
CO			
H_2			
CH_4			
N_2			
NO_2			
O_2			
SO_2			
H_2O			

Table 10.1: Information about ten gases.

b State which of the gases that you found in part a is not normally found in clean dry air.

....

c State which of the gases that you found in part a is the most abundant gas in clean dry air. Give the approximate percentage of this gas in clean dry air.

gas: ....   percentage: ....

d The names of *two* gases are not included in Figure 10.1. Add these names to Table 10.1.

e State which *two* gases in Table 10.1 are unreactive.

....

f Complete the final two columns of Table 10.1 by putting a tick (✓) in the correct rows.

TIP

Clean dry air does not contain any water vapour.

KEY WORDS

complete combustion: a type of combustion reaction in which a fuel is burned in a plentiful supply of oxygen; the complete combustion of hydrocarbon fuels produces only carbon dioxide and water.

desulfurisation: an industrial process for removing contaminating sulfur from fossil fuels such as petrol (gasoline) or diesel.

fossil fuels: fuels formed underground over geological periods of time from the remains of plants and animals; coal, oil and natural gas.

global warming: a long-term increase in the average temperature of the Earth's surface, which may be caused by human activities.

greenhouse effect: the natural phenomenon in which thermal energy from the Sun is 'trapped' at the Earth's surface by certain gases in the atmosphere (greenhouse gases).

Practice

2 **a** The boxes below show several gases, their environmental sources and their adverse effects. Draw lines to link each gas with its environmental sources and the adverse effect(s) which it causes. The first gas (methane) has been done for you.

Source	Gas	Adverse effect

Source

- motor vehicles
- farming
- power stations

Gas

- carbon dioxide
- carbon monoxide
- methane
- particulates
- oxides of nitrogen
- sulfur dioxide

Adverse effect

- toxic gas
- can cause respiratory problems
- causes acid rain
- causes global warming
- photochemical smog
- increased cancer risk

b State why carbon monoxide is toxic to humans.

....

c State which acids are produced from the gases you have identified as causing acid rain.

....

d Identify which gas is the second most abundant greenhouse gas in the atmosphere.

....

e Give *two* specific sources of the gas you identified in part d.

....

TIP

Although carbon dioxide is an essential part of clean air (0.04%), it is considered to be a pollutant if the percentage in the air increases.

KEY WORDS

greenhouse gas: a gas that absorbs heat reflected from the surface of the Earth, stopping it escaping the atmosphere.

particulates: very tiny solid particles produced during the combustion of fuels.

pollutants: substances, often harmful, which are added to another substance.

Challenge

3 Table 10.2 shows some methods, labelled from A to F, which could be used to reduce the quantities of pollutants in the atmosphere. Each method is linked with the gas or gases it is designed to help control.

A	Stop using fossil fuels to generate electricity. Use wind and solar power instead.	→	carbon dioxide
B	Stop using gas to heat homes. Use electricity instead.	→	carbon dioxide
C	React gases from power stations with calcium oxide (desulfurisation).	→	sulfur dioxide
D	Breed fewer cattle.	→	methane
E	Use electric vehicles instead of those powered by burning fossil fuels.	→	carbon dioxide, carbon monoxide, particulates and oxides of nitrogen
F	Use catalytic converters to clean exhaust gases from cars and other vehicles.	→	carbon monoxide and oxides of nitrogen

Table 10.2: Methods of reducing atmospheric pollutants.

a State which *two* methods from Table 10.2 would have the greatest effect on global warming. Explain your answer.

....

....

....

b State which *two* methods would be easiest to implement. Explain your answer.

....

....

....

c Explain why your answers demonstrate the problems of tackling air pollution.

....

....

....

....

4 The fuel for petrol and diesel vehicles does not contain any nitrogenous compounds.

    a Explain why the exhaust gases from such vehicles contain harmful oxides of nitrogen (NO_x).

       ....

       ....

       ....

       ....

    b Modern vehicles are fitted with catalytic converters to remove oxides of nitrogen and carbon monoxide. Complete the following symbol equation for one of the reactions that takes place in a catalytic converter.

       $2CO(g) + 2NO(g) \rightarrow$ _____ + _____

    c Identify what type of agent the nitrogen(II) oxide acts as in this equation.

       ....

Exercise 10.2

IN THIS EXERCISE YOU WILL:

- describe carbon dioxide and methane as greenhouse gases

- investigate how levels of carbon dioxide are linked to increased global warming

- extrapolate data from a graph to make predictions about climate change

- investigate the causes and effects of global warming and strategies to reduce the effects of these environmental issues

- describe how greenhouse gases cause global warming.

Focus

1 Use the words provided to complete the text.

        atmosphere   carbon dioxide   gases   global warming

        greenhouse   industrial   life   methane   water   weather

    The _____ effect has kept the Earth at a temperature suitable for the

    development of _____ for many thousands of years.

As _____ activity has increased during the 20th and 21st centuries, more and more greenhouse gases have been released into the _____. Carbon dioxide and methane are the two _____ causing the greatest problem. _____ is 25 times more potent as a greenhouse gas but _____ is present in greater quantities. Because of these gases, more of the heat from the Sun is kept within the Earth's atmosphere. This causes _____. Much of this heat warms _____ in the oceans, which cover about 70% of the Earth's surface. Increased temperatures in the oceans and in the atmosphere have an effect on the Earth's climate. This effect means that extreme _____ events are more likely.

Practice

2   The data in Table 10.3 show the concentration of carbon dioxide in the atmosphere from 1880 to 2020. The table also shows the mean average temperature of the Earth over the same period.

Year	CO_2 concentration / ppm	Mean average temperature / °C	Year	CO_2 concentration / ppm	Mean average temperature / °C
1880	290	13.9	1992	356	14.1
1900	297	13.9	1996	361	14.3
1920	303	13.8	2000	369	14.4
1940	309	14.1	2004	377	14.6
1960	317	14.0	2008	385	14.5
1980	338	14.3	2012	394	14.6
1984	343	14.1	2016	403	14.7
1988	351	14.4	2020	413	14.9

Table 10.3: Atmospheric carbon dioxide concentration and mean temperature of the Earth from 1880 to 2020.

a On the grid provided, plot two graphs to show the variation of carbon dioxide (left axis) and temperature (right axis) between 1880 and 2020.

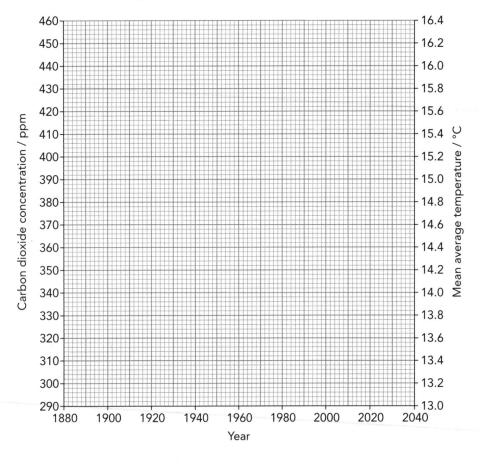

TIP

When drawing two graphs on the same axes, use a different symbol for each variable. For example, you might use a cross (×) for one variable and a dot in a circle (⊙) for the other variable. Identify each variable using a key or label.

b Describe the trends in carbon dioxide level and mean average temperature from 1880 to 2020.

i Carbon dioxide level:

....

....

ii Mean temperature:

....

....

c   Between 1988 and 1992, the mean average temperature of the Earth decreased.
    Does this mean that the global atmosphere is not warming? Explain your answer.

    ....

    ....

d   Using your graph, predict the likely quantity of carbon dioxide and the likely
    mean average temperature in 2040.

    ....

Challenge

3   Figure 10.2 is an incomplete mind map showing the causes and effects of
    global warming.

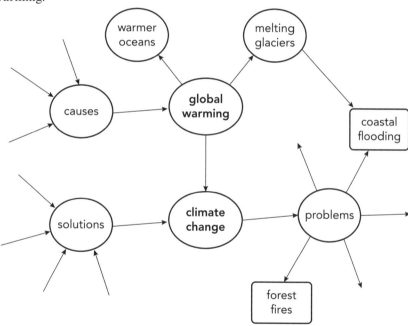

Figure 10.2: Mind map for global warming and climate change.

a   Why would melting glaciers lead to coastal flooding?

    ....

b   Why might lack of rain cause more forest fires?

    ....

c   Complete the mind map by adding:

- more of the problems caused by climate change
- a number of causes of global warming
- some ways in which the problems of climate change might be solved.

PEER ASSESSMENT

Compare your mind map with others in your group. Try to produce a combined version using the best parts of each student's map. What features did all of the completed mind maps have in common? Did you miss any important features from your mind map?

4   Use the words provided to complete the description of the greenhouse effect.

absorbed	activities	atmosphere	climate	energy	oceans
gases	global	infrared	loss	methane	natural
radiated	re-emit	reflected	Sun	temperature	trapping

The greenhouse effect is a _____ phenomenon that warms the surface

of the Earth. When thermal _____ (_____ radiation) from the

_____ reaches the Earth's _____, around 30% is _____

back to space and around 70% is _____ by the oceans and land to heat the

planet. Some of this heat is then _____ back up into the atmosphere.

Greenhouse _____ in the atmosphere – such as carbon dioxide and

_____ – can absorb this infrared radiation and then _____ it back

toward the Earth. This reduces heat _____ to space and keeps the Earth's

_____ warm enough to sustain life.

Human _____ are increasing the amount of greenhouse gases released

into the atmosphere, _____ extra heat and causing _____

temperatures to rise. This warming of both the atmosphere and the _____

gives rise to the different aspects of _____ change.

> Water

Exercise 10.3

IN THIS EXERCISE YOU WILL:

- investigate how water is purified during water treatment
- describe different ways of testing for the presence and purity of water
- explain why distilled water is used in preference to ordinary tap water in practical chemistry experiments.

Focus

1   Drinking water is often obtained from rivers. River water may contain a mixture of the following impurities:

A	twigs and leaves
B	plastic bags and bottles
C	organic chemicals with a strong odour
D	metals and minerals dissolved from rocks and other sources
E	sewage and animal waste
F	bacteria and other microbes from sewage

River water is treated to make it suitable for drinking. State which impurity (A–F) is treated by the following processes.

a   sedimentation and filtration ....

b   carbon to remove tastes and smells ....

c   chlorination ....

Practice

2   Explain why distilled water is used in preference to ordinary tap water in practical chemistry experiments.

....

....

....

3 a   Outline *two* ways in which we can test for the presence of water.

....

....

  b   Outline how we can test the purity of water.

....

....

Challenge

4   Most countries in the world have areas where there is no piped water supply.
    People in these areas have to rely on water from rivers, streams or wells.

   •   Water from wells is usually less polluted than water from rivers.

   •   All untreated water can contain harmful microbes.

   •   Boiling water kills most harmful microbes.

   •   Treated water can be supplied in bottles or tanks.

   •   Chemical tablets can be added to water to kill harmful microbes.

   •   People use water for many different things (e.g. watering crops, washing,
       cooking, flushing toilets, drinking).

  a   State why water from wells is usually less polluted than water from rivers.

....

  b   Explain whether pure (treated) water is needed for all of the different uses.

....

....

  c   State why it is not necessary to use treated water when boiling food
      during cooking.

....

  d   Bottled water is often supplied for drinking. State why this is bad for
      the environment.

....

> Chapter 11
Organic chemistry

> Formulae, functional groups and terminology, and naming organic compounds

Exercise 11.1

IN THIS EXERCISE YOU WILL:

- investigate the hydrocarbons and identify saturated and unsaturated hydrocarbons

- name and draw the displayed and structural formulae of members of the alkanes, alkenes and alcohols.

KEY WORDS

functional group: the atom or group of atoms responsible for the characteristic reactions of a compound.

homologous series: a family of similar compounds with similar chemical properties due to the presence of the same functional group.

hydrocarbons: organic compounds that contain carbon and hydrogen only; the alkanes and alkenes are two series of hydrocarbons.

Focus

1   Use the words provided to complete the text about compounds containing carbon and hydrogen. Not all of the words are used.

alkanes   alkenes   bromine   petroleum   ethane   ethene   hydrogen

methane   propane   chains   chlorine   colourless   double

The chief source of organic compounds is the naturally occurring mixture of

hydrocarbons known as _____. Hydrocarbons are compounds that

contain carbon and _____ only. There are many hydrocarbons because

carbon atoms can join together to form long _____.

There is a series of hydrocarbons with single covalent bonds only between the
carbon atoms in the molecule. These hydrocarbons are saturated and they are

called _____. The simplest of these saturated hydrocarbons has the

formula CH_4 and is called _____.

Unsaturated hydrocarbons can also occur. These molecules contain at least one carbon–carbon _____ bond. These compounds belong to the _____, a second series of hydrocarbons. The simplest of this 'family' of unsaturated hydrocarbons has the formula C_2H_4 and is known as _____. The test for an unsaturated hydrocarbon is to add the sample to _____ water. If the hydrocarbon is unsaturated, the bromine water will change colour from orange–brown to _____.

KEY WORDS

saturated hydrocarbons: hydrocarbon molecules in which all the carbon–carbon bonds are single covalent bonds.

structural formula: a representation of an organic molecule showing how all the groups of atoms are arranged in the structure; for example, the structural formula of ethanol is CH_3CH_2OH.

unsaturated hydrocarbons: hydrocarbons whose molecules contain at least one carbon–carbon double or triple bond.

2 Table 11.1 shows the names, formulae and boiling points of the first members of the family of unsaturated hydrocarbons.

a Complete Table 11.1.

Name	Formula	Boiling point/ °C
	C_2H_4	−102
propene	C_3H_6	−48
butene	C_4H_8	−7
pentene		

Table 11.1: The first members of the series of unsaturated hydrocarbons.

b Deduce the general formula of members of the series of compounds shown in Table 11.1. Use *n* to represent the number of carbon atoms in the molecule.

....

c This family of compounds is an example of a homologous series. State what is meant by the term homologous series.

....

....

d Name the functional group that gives this series its characteristic chemical properties.

....

Practice

3 The full structure of an organic compound can be represented by its displayed formula. Table 11.2 shows the molecular and displayed formulae of members of several homologous series.

Complete Table 11.2.

Name of compound	Homologous series	Molecular formula	Displayed formula
propanol			H—C—C—C—O—H (with H atoms shown on carbons)
propene		C_3H_6	
ethanol	alcohols		H—C—C—O—H (with H atoms shown on carbons)
ethane	alkanes	C_2H_6	

Table 11.2: Information about different organic compounds.

SELF ASSESSMENT

Look at your answers to question 3 and use the following definitions to check your answers:

- **alcohols:** a series of organic compounds containing the functional group –OH and with the general formula $C_nH_{2n+1}OH$

- **alkanes:** a series of hydrocarbons with the general formula C_nH_{2n+2}; they are saturated molecules, as they have only single bonds between carbon atoms in their structure

- **alkenes:** a series of hydrocarbons with the general formula C_nH_{2n}; they are unsaturated molecules, as they have a C=C double bond somewhere in the chain

With a partner, discuss the difference between a molecular formula and a displayed formula. What clear, additional information is given by the displayed formula that is not obvious in the molecular formula? Is this clear in the displayed formulae you have drawn?

Challenge

4 A molecule of an organic compound can be represented by two other types of formulae. These formulae give useful information about the composition of the compound.

The structural formula of a molecule shows how the groups are arranged but is simpler than the full displayed formula. Table 11.3 shows the molecular and structural formulae of some typical compounds.

Complete Table 11.3.

Compound	Molecular formula	Structural formula
butane	C_4H_{10}	
propene	C_3H_6	$CH_3CH=CH_2$
ethanol	C_2H_5OH	

Table 11.3: The molecular and structural formulae of some organic compounds.

5 But-2-ene has the structural formula $CH_3CH=CHCH_3$. Give the name and structural formula of another molecule with the same molecular formula but a different structure.

....

....

Exercise 11.2

IN THIS EXERCISE YOU WILL:

- define homologous series
- describe the general characteristics of a homologous series.

Focus

1 There are several different homologous series, each with a distinctive functional group in the molecule.

   a Define *homologous series*.

   ....

   ....

b   State the general characteristics of a homologous series.

....

....

2   State the homologous series to which the following compounds belong.

a   butane ....

b   propanol ....

c   heptane ....

Practice

3   It is possible to deduce the name and molecular formula of a compound if you know the homologous series to which it belongs and the number of carbon atoms present.

Give the name of the following compounds.

a   the alkane with one carbon atom: ....

b   the alkene with two carbon atoms: ....

c   the alcohol with two carbon atoms: ....

Challenge

4   Homologous series show a trend in physical properties.

a   Use the data in Table 11.4 to identify the compound which is not part of the homologous series.

Compound	Number of carbons	Boiling point/°C
A	1	−162
B	2	78
C	3	−42
D	4	−0.5
E	5	36

Table 11.4: Data about five organic compounds.

b   Deduce a possible boiling point for the compound which should be present in the homologous series, instead of the compound you identified in part a. Justify your answer.

....

....

> Alkanes, alkenes and alcohols
Exercise 11.3

IN THIS EXERCISE YOU WILL:

- investigate the characteristic reactions of members of different homologous series

- distinguish between saturated and unsaturated hydrocarbons by observing the presence or absence of double bonds in their displayed formulae

- describe how unsaturated hydrocarbons are much more reactive than saturated hydrocarbons as they can take part in addition reactions

- describe addition reactions of unsaturated hydrocarbons

- describe the process of cracking.

KEY WORDS

addition reaction: a reaction in which a simple molecule adds across the carbon–carbon double bond of an alkene.

fuel: a substance that can be used as a source of energy, usually by burning (combustion).

Focus

1   **a**   Table 11.5 shows information about two hydrocarbons. Both molecules have a structure involving two carbon atoms. (A_r: H = 1, C = 12)

Complete Table 11.5.

Name	ethane	ethene
Molecular formula	C_2H_6	
Saturated / unsaturated		
Displayed formula		
Relative molecular mass		

Table 11.5: Information about two hydrocarbons.

b   Explain why each hydrocarbon is saturated or unsaturated.

i   ethane: ....

....

ii   ethene: ....

....

c Ethene belongs to a homologous series. Name this homologous series and identify the functional group present.

....

Practice

2 Limonene is a colourless unsaturated hydrocarbon found in oranges and lemons. The structure of limonene is shown in Figure 11.1.

a On Figure 11.1, draw a circle around the bonds which make limonene an unsaturated hydrocarbon.

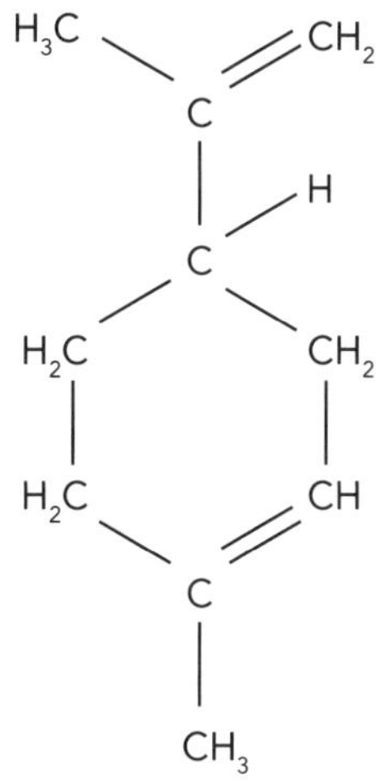

Figure 11.1: Structure of limonene.

b State the molecular formula of limonene.

....

c Calculate the relative molecular mass of limonene.

....

d Describe the colour change which occurs when excess limonene is added to a few drops of bromine water.

....

3 **a** In the space provided, draw the displayed formula for ethanol (an alcohol).

> **TIP**
>
> You have studied several examples of each type of compound (such as alkanes, alkenes, alcohols, etc.). You should develop the ability to apply this knowledge to compounds that you may not have seen before. Do not be distracted by the unusual details; instead, focus on the features that are common to both examples.

b The general formula for the alcohols is $C_nH_{2n+1}OH$. Give the formula for the alcohol with three carbons.

....

c Calculate the relative molecular mass of the alcohol in part b. (A_r: C = 12, H = 1, O = 16)

....

4 Use bullet points to describe the key features of cracking. Describe the conditions for the reaction and outline the products.

....

....

....

....

Challenge

5   There are many compounds with the formula C_4H_8. Figure 11.2 shows the partial displayed formulae of two of these compounds.

   a   Complete the two displayed formulae in Figure 11.2 by adding the hydrogen atoms.

C=C–C–C   C–C=C–C

Figure 11.2: Displayed formulae of two compounds with the formula C_4H_8.

   b   In the space, draw the displayed formulae of the compounds formed when the compounds shown in Figure 11.2 react with bromine.

6   Alkenes undergo addition reactions.

   a   Complete these reactions, giving the products and conditions:

      i   ethene + bromine → ....

      ii   ethene + hydrogen → .... conditions: ....

      iii   ethene + steam → .... conditions: ....

   b   Draw the structural and displayed formulae of the products of reactions i to iii.

Exercise 11.4

IN THIS EXERCISE YOU WILL:

- describe the combustion and uses of alcohols.

Focus

1   Butan-1-ol takes part in the characteristic reactions of alcohols.
    Balance the equation for the complete combustion of butan-1-ol.

$C_4H_9OH + ...O_2 \rightarrow ....CO_2 + ...H_2O$

Practice

2   Ethanol is a good fuel. It burns with a clear flame and gives out lots of heat.
    It is also a liquid at room temperature and so it is easily transported.

   a   Give the symbol equation for the complete combustion of ethanol.

   ....

   b   State the products of the incomplete combustion of ethanol.

   ....

   c   Give *five* reasons why ethanol is a good fuel.

   ....

   ....

   ....

   ....

   ....

Challenge

3   Alcohols are a homologous series which have similar chemical properties and a gradual change in physical properties. The use of an alcohol as a fuel depends on the amount of alcohol vapour present; this in turn depends on the boiling point of the alcohol. Table 11.6 shows the boiling points of some straight-chain alcohols.

Name of alcohol	Structure	Relative molecular mass of alcohol (C = 12, H = 1, O = 16)	Boiling point/ °C
methanol	CH_3OH	32	65
A:	CH_3CH_2OH	46	78
propan-1-ol	$CH_3CH_2CH_2OH$	60	D:
butan-1-ol	$CH_3CH_2CH_2CH_2OH$	74	118
pentan-1-ol	B:	C:	138

Table 11.6: Some straight-chain alcohols.

a   Complete the table by filling in the gaps labelled A, B and C.

b   Imagine you have been given some graph paper and the data in Table 11.6. Explain how you would use the data to estimate the boiling point of an alcohol using a graph. Your explanation should include the following:
   - what you would plot as the independent variable and what you would use as the dependent variable
   - how you would plot the graph
   - how you would use the graph to estimate the boiling points of propan-1-ol (gap D in Table 11.6) and hexan-1-ol.

   ....

   ....

   ....

   ....

   ....

   ....

c   Explain which of your estimates you would be less confident about – propan-1-ol or hexan-1-ol.

   ....

   ....

   ....

› Fuels

Exercise 11.5

IN THIS EXERCISE YOU WILL:

- discuss the fractions obtained from the distillation of petroleum and their major uses

- plot a bar chart and interpret data from the chart

- show how catalytic cracking can be used to produce shorter alkanes and alkenes from the larger alkanes of the lower fractions.

KEY WORDS

fractional distillation: a method of distillation using a fractionating column to separate liquids with different boiling points.

petroleum (or crude oil): a fossil fuel formed underground over many millions of years by conditions of high pressure and temperature acting on the remains of dead sea creatures.

Focus

Petroleum (crude oil) is a raw material which is processed in an oil refinery. Two of the processes used are:

- fractional distillation
- catalytic cracking.

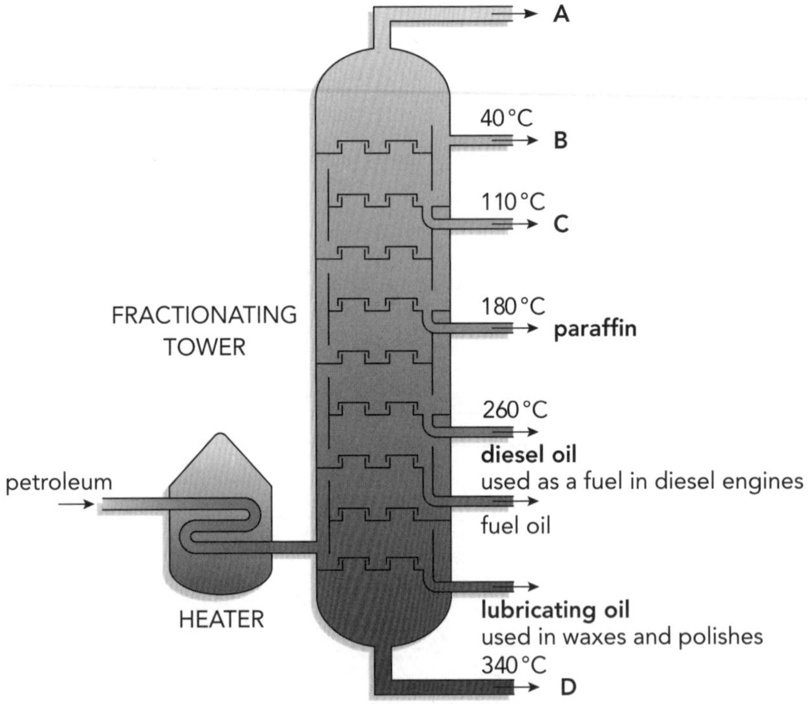

Figure 11.3: The fractional distillation of petroleum.

1 Figure 11.3 shows the fractional distillation of petroleum. Give the name and a major use for each of the fractions labelled A–D.

A ....

B ....

C ....

D ....

2 a State which physical property is used to separate petroleum by fractional distillation.

....

b State how the chain length and boiling points of the fractions vary as you move up the fractionating tower.

....

....

Practice

3 Table 11.7 gives information about the proportions of certain fractions in a sample of petroleum from a particular oil-producing region. It also shows the commercial demand for these fractions.

Fraction	Number of carbon atoms per molecule	Proportion in petroleum / %	Percentage needed by the oil refinery to supply demand / %
A	1–4	2	5
B	4–12	8	22
C	7–14	10	5
paraffin	12–16	16	11
diesel oil	14–18	19	23
fuel oil, waxes and D	over 20	45	34

Table 11.7: Supply and demand for the different fractions from the distillation of petroleum.

a   On the grid provided, plot a bar chart showing the proportion and percentage needed for each fraction in Table 11.7.

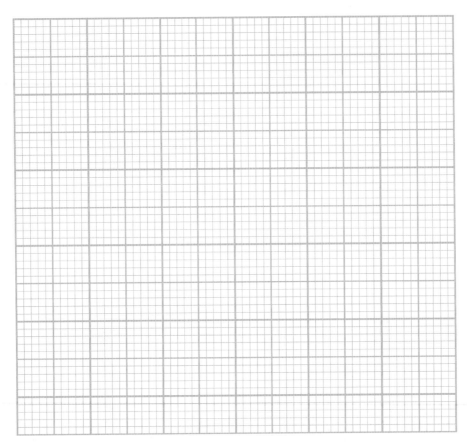

As you can see, there are differences between availability and demand for the different fractions. There is a need to manipulate the chemistry of the fractions.

b   State which fractions are in the greatest demand generally.

....

c   Calculate the total proportion of the demand that is used for fuelling cars and lorries (trucks).

....

Representing data in a bar chart is not as common in chemistry as drawing a line graph but it is an important skill. Use the checklist in Table 11.8 to assess the bar chart you drew in question 3a.

For each point, award yourself:

- **2 marks** if you did it really well

- **1 mark**   if you made a good attempt at it and partly succeeded

- **0 marks** if you did not try to do it, or did not succeed.

Checklist	Marks awarded
Have you drawn the axes with a ruler, using most of the width and height of the grid?	
Have you made clear which bars show the proportion in petroleum and which show the percentage in demand?	
Have you labelled the axes correctly?	
Have you used an appropriate scale for each of your axes?	
Have you drawn your bars clearly and plotted the data correctly?	
Total (out of 10):	

Take a look at the marks you gave yourself. What did you do well? What aspects will you focus on next time?

Challenge

4   The hydrocarbon $C_{15}H_{32}$ can be cracked to make propene and one other hydrocarbon.

   a   Write an equation for this reaction.

   ....

   b   Draw the displayed formula of propene.

> Polymers

Exercise 11.6

IN THIS EXERCISE YOU WILL:

- investigate polymerisation using the synthesis of poly(ethene) as an example of addition polymerisation

- deduce the repeat unit of an addition polymer

- compare addition and condensation polymers.

Focus

1   Poly(ethene) is a polymer. It is used to make plastic for a wide variety of containers.

   a   Use the words provided to complete the text about poly(ethene). Not all of the words are used.

   acids   addition   condensation   ethane

   monomers   polymer   polymerisation   ethene

   Poly(ethene) is an _____ polymer formed from many _____

   molecules. In this reaction, the starting molecules can be described as

   _____. The process is known as _____.

   b   Draw the structure of poly(ethene) showing at least *three* repeat units.

KEY WORDS

addition polymer: a polymer formed by an addition reaction; the monomer molecules contain a C=C double bond.

condensation polymer: a polymer formed by a condensation reaction – e.g. nylon is produced by the condensation reaction between 1,6-diaminohexane and hexanedioic acid; this is the type of polymerisation used in biological systems to produce proteins, nucleic acids and polysaccharides.

monomer: a small molecule, such as ethene, which can be polymerised to make a polymer.

polyamide: a polymer where the repeating units are joined together by amide (peptide) links, e.g. nylon and proteins.

polymer: a substance consisting of very large molecules made by polymerising a large number of repeating units (monomers).

polymerisation: the chemical reaction in which molecules (monomers) join together to form a long-chain polymer.

Practice

2 Addition polymerisation is a method of making polymers from unsaturated monomers. Other synthetic polymers, such as nylon and PET, are made by a different type of polymerisation involving condensation rather than addition reactions. Table 11.8 lists the main differences between these two types of polymerisation.

Use the words provided to complete the comparisons in Table 11.8.

an addition   a condensation   double   functional   hydrolysed

polymer   two   unsaturated   water   one

	Addition polymerisation	Condensation polymerisation
monomers used	usually many molecules of a single _____ monomer, containing a carbon–carbon _____ bond	molecules of _____ different monomers are usually used; monomers contain a reactive _____ group at each end of the molecule
reaction taking place	_____ reaction	_____ reaction with loss of a small molecule (usually _____) each time a monomer joins the chain
nature of product	only _____ product formed – the polymer	two products formed: the _____ plus another, small, molecule
	non-biodegradable	can be biodegradable
	resistant to acids	PET can be _____ back to monomers by acids or alkalis

Table 11.8: Comparing addition and condensation polymerisation.

Challenge

3 Figure 11.4 shows the structure of a different addition polymer, X.

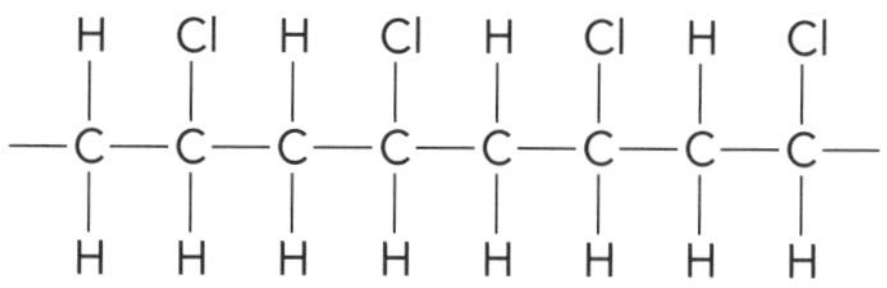

Figure 11.4: The structure of polymer X.

Draw the structure of the monomer from which polymer X is formed.

TIP

When drawing a representation of the structure of a polymer (whether an addition or condensation type), remember to show the continuation bonds at both ends (as in Figure 11.4).

4   There are various types of important condensation polymer. In each case, the reaction to form the polymer can be represented by a schematic diagram. This diagram shows only the key interactions between the functional groups and the nature of the linkage involved.

H_2N —☐— NH_2 HOOC —▨— COOH

Figure 11.5: Possible monomers for a condensation polymer.

a   What type of polymer can be formed from the monomers represented in Figure 11.5?

Choose from: polyamide, polyester or polysaccharide.

....

b   Draw the structure of the polymer formed, showing at least three monomers joined together.

c   Name the molecule that is eliminated at the formation of each linkage.

....

d   Give the name of the most important synthetic polymer of this type.

....

Chapter 12

Experimental techniques and chemical analysis

> Experimental design

Exercise 12.1

IN THIS EXERCISE YOU WILL:

- investigate the effect of concentration on rate of reaction

- identify appropriate apparatus for measuring variables

- draw a graph from data and analyse the results

- design an experiment to determine the effect of temperature on rate of reaction.

KEY WORDS

volumetric pipette: a pipette used to measure out a volume of solution accurately.

Focus

When sodium thiosulfate reacts with hydrochloric acid, the following reaction takes place:

$Na_2S_2O_3(aq) + 2HCl(aq) \rightarrow 2NaCl(aq) + H_2O(aq) + SO_2(g) + S(s)$

At low temperatures, the sulfur dioxide remains dissolved in the water. However, sulfur is a solid and it forms a pale yellow precipitate in the solution.

The flask containing the reaction mixture can be placed over a cross (✗) drawn on a piece of paper (as shown in Figure 12.1). Eventually, the precipitate of sulfur particles turns the liquid so cloudy that the cross is hidden. The length of time taken for the cross to 'disappear' can be used to measure the rate of reaction.

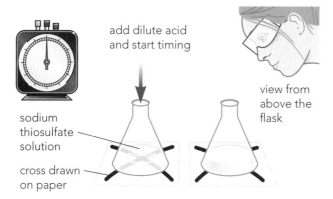

add dilute acid and start timing

view from above the flask

sodium thiosulfate solution

cross drawn on paper

Figure 12.1: The 'disappearing cross' experiment.

A student followed these instructions to perform an experiment:

- Measure $30\,cm^3$ of sodium thiosulfate and add to the flask on the paper.

- Rapidly add $10\,cm^3$ of hydrochloric acid to the flask. Immediately start the timer.

- Stop the timer when the cross on the paper can no longer be seen.

- Record the time taken.

- Empty and rinse the flask.

- Repeat the experiment using $25\,cm^3$ of sodium thiosulfate and $5\,cm^3$ of water.

- Repeat four more times. Reduce the volume of sodium thiosulfate by $5\,cm^3$ each time. Increase the volume of water by $5\,cm^3$ each time.

The student's experimental results are shown in Table 12.1.

Experiment	Volume of acid / cm³	Volume of sodium thiosulfate / cm³	Volume of water / cm³	Time for cross to disappear / s
1	10	30	0	35
2	10	25	5	42
3	10	20	10	50
4	10	15	15	60
5	10	10	20	100
6	10	5	25	250

Table 12.1: Results from disappearing cross reaction.

1 State which piece of apparatus – a measuring cylinder or a volumetric pipette – would be better for adding the acid to the mixture. Give a reason for your answer.

....

....

....

2   On the grid provided, plot a graph of time taken for the cross to disappear against volume of sodium thiosulfate solution used. Use the results in Table 12.1.

Practice

3   **a**   Use your graph to estimate the volume of sodium thiosulfate that would give a time of 70 seconds.

....

b   Calculate what volume of water would have to be added if this experiment was carried out.

....

....

> **TIP**
>
> It is important to interpret the shape of graphs from rate experiments. Think about what the shape of the graph tells you about the relationship between rate of reaction and reactant concentration.

Challenge

4   This reaction between sodium thiosulfate and hydrochloric acid can also be used to find the effect of temperature on rate of reaction.

    a   Describe how you would carry out this investigation. Identify any additional apparatus you would need and explain how you would make the investigation a fair test (by controlling all variables other than temperature and rate of reaction).

....

....

....

....

....

....

....

....

    b   Sulfur dioxide is a toxic gas. Explain why you must not heat the reaction mixture to a temperature in excess of 50 °C.

....

....

SELF ASSESSMENT

Look at your description of how you would carry out an investigation (question **4a**). Use this checklist to assess your description.
Have you included:

- additional apparatus needed

- safety considerations

- what measurements you would take and when you would take them

- details of any repeat measurements you would take

- an explanation of how you would ensure the experiment was a fair test (a clear study of how reaction rate varies with temperature)?

› Separation and purification
Exercise 12.2

IN THIS EXERCISE YOU WILL:

- discuss the differences between elements, mixtures and compounds
- consider a variety of methods used to separate different mixtures
- show how melting point and boiling point can be used to assess the purity of a substance
- design an experiment to determine the composition of an alloy.

Focus

1 a   Write each of these substances in the correct column in Table 12.2.

aluminium   brass   carbon dioxide   copper sulfate

dilute nitric acid   methane   seawater   sodium   zinc

Element	Mixture	Compound

Table 12.2: Elements, compounds and mixtures.

  b   State which type of substance (element, mixture or compound) consists of two or more elements and cannot be separated into different substances. Explain your answer.

....

....

KEY WORDS

distillation: the process of boiling a liquid and then condensing the vapour produced back into a liquid; used to purify liquids and to separate liquids from solutions.

filtration: the process of separating a solid from a liquid, using a fine filter paper which does not allow the solid to pass through.

solvent: the liquid that dissolves a solid solute to form a solution; water is the most common solvent; other liquids in organic chemistry that can act as solvents are called organic solvents.

Practice

2 Mixtures can be separated into their different components in a number of ways, including:

- crystallisation
- filtration
- fractional distillation
- simple distillation
- use of a solvent.

a State which method could be used to separate pure water from seawater.

....

b Give an example of a mixture that could be separated by filtration. Identify the filtrate and the residue from this mixture.

mixture: ....

filtrate: ....

residue: ....

c Identify the *three* methods that would be used to separate a mixture of salt and sand.

....

3 Describe how crystallisation can be used to separate copper sulfate crystals from a solution of copper sulfate.

....

....

....

Challenge

4 Explain the difference between simple distillation and fractional distillation. Your answer should include examples of how each method is used.

....

....

....

....

5 Describe how you could use melting point and boiling point to test the purity of:

a water

....

b a metal.

....

6 Brass is an alloy made from a mixture of copper and zinc. Zinc dissolves in hydrochloric acid but copper does not. You are given a sample of powdered brass. Design an experiment to find how much of the brass is copper and how much is zinc.

....

....

....

....

....

....

....

....

> **TIP**
>
> The presence of an impurity in a substance increases the difference between the melting and boiling points of the substance: this makes the melting point lower and the boiling point higher. The impurity also makes these temperatures less precise.

> Chromatography

Exercise 12.3

IN THIS EXERCISE YOU WILL:

- examine how a simple chromatogram should be set up
- practise different ways of interpreting simple chromatograms
- calculate the R_f value.

KEY WORDS

chromatogram: the result of a paper chromatography run, showing where the spots of the samples have moved to.

chromatography: a technique used to separate mixtures of dissolved substances; originally used to separate coloured dyes.

R_f value: in chromatography, the ratio of the distance travelled by the solute to the distance travelled by the solvent front.

Focus

The chromatogram in Figure 12.2 compares two coloured mixtures, X and Y.

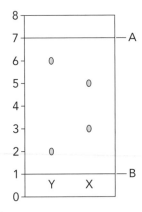

Figure 12.2: An experimental chromatogram.

1   Describe what is shown by the two lines A and B.

A   ....

B   ....

2   The chromatography paper is 8 cm long. State the level of the solvent at the start of the chromatography.

    ....

TIP

Chromatography can be used to identify unknown substances by comparison with known substances. It can also be used to identify pure and impure substances.

3 Line B was drawn in pencil. Explain why.

....

....

....

4 State whether substances X and Y have any components in common. Explain your answer.

....

Practice

5 Identify which component of mixture X is the most soluble in the solvent used. Explain your answer.

....

....

6 Explain how chromatography can be used to identify whether a substance is pure or impure.

....

....

Challenge

7 Substances can be identified by measuring their R_f value. Calculate the R_f value of the component in mixture Y which moved the smaller distance. Give your answer to two decimal places.

....

....

KEY EQUATION
$$R_f = \frac{\text{distance travelled by substance}}{\text{distance travelled by solvent}}$$

> Identification of ions and gases

Exercise 12.4

IN THIS EXERCISE YOU WILL:

- describe the colours seen in flame tests for the following metal cations: Li^+, Na^+, K^+, Ca^{2+}

- consider the tests used to identify different cations and anions

- discuss how to interpret the results of these tests for ions.

KEY WORDS

flame test: testing a compound by holding a sample in a flame to discover which colour, if any, is produced.

limewater: a solution of calcium hydroxide in water; it is an alkali and is used in the test for carbon dioxide gas.

precipitation: the sudden formation of a solid, either when two solutions are mixed or when a gas is bubbled into a solution.

Focus

1 Complete Table 12.3 to identify the flame test colour given by each cation.

Cation (metal ion)	Colour of flame
lithium, Li^+	
sodium, Na^+	
potassium, K^+	
copper(II), Cu^{2+}	

Table 12.3: Flame test colours for metal cations.

2 Carbonates are used as antacids. You are given three antacids: A, B and C. One antacid contains sodium carbonate, one antacid contains calcium carbonate, and the other antacid contains both sodium carbonate and calcium carbonate.

Describe how you could use a flame test to discover which antacid contains which carbonate(s).

Your answer should include how to perform the test and how you would interpret the results.

....

....

....

....

....

Practice

3   A student tested the three antacids A–C using the flame test. One test gave a correct result for calcium ions, but the other two tests both gave a positive result for sodium ions. Sodium ions give a bright yellow colour which hides the colours from other ions. Describe how you could use sodium hydroxide solution to discover which of the antacids contained both sodium and calcium ions.

....

....

....

....

4   You have two samples. One is potassium nitrate and the other is potassium carbonate.

a   Give the formula of each compound.

....

b   Describe the tests you would use to identify which compound is which.

....

....

....

....

....

....

Challenge

5   A student was given a mixture of four ions. The ions were: Ca^{2+}, CO_3^{2-}, NH_4^+ and Cl^-. They carried out the following procedure:

A   Add distilled water to the mixture and stir.

B   Filter the mixture.

C   Dry the residue, then add hydrochloric acid. – Fizzing was observed and a gas was produced which turned limewater cloudy.

D   Dissolve the residue into the acid and carry out a flame test on the solution. – A brick-red flame was observed.

E Divide the filtrate from B into two portions. Test the portions separately for the ammonium ion and the chloride ion. Positive results were obtained.

    a Identify the two ions present in the residue.

    ....

    b Explain how the results tell you this.

    ....

    ....

    ....

    ....

    c Name the compound forming the residue.

    ....

    ....

6   **a** The test for the ammonium ion (step E) involved heating the filtrate with sodium hydroxide. Identify the two observations that would confirm the presence of the ammonium ion.

    ....

    ....

    ....

    b The test for the chloride ion (step E) involved the use of silver nitrate solution and an acid. Name this acid.

    ....

    c State what the student observed that confirmed the presence of chloride ions.

    ....

    d Give the ionic equation for the reaction between chloride ions and silver nitrate solution. Include state symbols.

    ....

e Name the compound present in the filtrate.

....

f Give the balanced symbol equation for the reaction of this compound with sodium hydroxide.

....

Exercise 12.5

IN THIS EXERCISE YOU WILL:

- consider the tests used to identify different aqueous cations
- discuss how to interpret the results of these tests
- consider the tests used to identify common gases
- discuss how to interpret the results of some of these tests.

Focus

1 The tests for transition metal cations iron (Fe^{2+} and Fe^{3+}) and copper (Cu^{2+}) involve precipitation reactions. Identify which of these cations would give the following test results.

    a a light blue precipitate with aqueous ammonia: ....

    b a green precipitate with aqueous ammonia which then turns brown on

    standing: ....

2 **a** Name the gas which is identified using limewater. ....

    b Explain how the test for this gas is carried out.

    test: ....

    result: ....

    c Describe the tests used and the observations for oxygen gas and hydrogen gas.

      i test for oxygen: ....

      observations: ....

      ii test for hydrogen: ....

      observations: ....

Practice

3 The green precipitate produced in the test in question 1b turns brown on standing. Explain why this happens and state what type of reaction is taking place.

....

....

Challenge

4 A mixture of powdered crystals contains both ammonium ions (NH_4^+) and zinc ions (Zn^{2+}).

The two salts contain the same anion. Table 12.4 shows the results of tests carried out by a student.

a Complete Table 12.4 to describe the observations made by the student.

Test	Observations
1 A sample of the solid mixture was dissolved in distilled water. The solution was acidified with dilute HCl(aq) and a solution of $BaCl_2$ was added.	A white precipitate was formed.
2 A sample of the solid was placed in a test-tube. NaOH(aq) was added and the mixture warmed. A piece of moist red litmus paper was held at the mouth of the tube.	The solid dissolved and pungent fumes were given off. The litmus paper turned ...., indicating the presence of .... ions.
3 A sample of the solid was dissolved in distilled water to give a .... solution. NaOH(aq) was added dropwise until in excess.	A .... precipitate was formed which was .... in excess alkali.
4 A further sample of the solid was dissolved in distilled water. Concentrated ammonia solution (NH_3(aq)) was added dropwise until in excess.	A .... precipitate was formed. On addition of excess alkali, the precipitate was ....

Table 12.4: Analytical tests on a mixture of substances.

b Give the names and formulae of the *two* salts in the mixture.

....

....

c Give the name and formula of the precipitate formed in tests 3 and 4.

....

5 a The tests for ammonia and chlorine both use damp litmus paper. Describe what happens to the litmus paper in each case.

ammonia: ....

chlorine: ....

b Carbon dioxide is an acidic gas. State why litmus paper is not used to test for it.

....

....

SELF ASSESSMENT

Tick (✓) the boxes in the table to show what you can do. Then think about how you can improve your understanding in any areas that need more work.

I can	Needs more work	Almost there	Ready to move on
understand the tests for ions			
understand why the tests are useful			
understand why more than one test is sometimes needed.			

> Acid–base titrations

Exercise 12.6

IN THIS EXERCISE YOU WILL:

- consider the apparatus necessary to carry out a titration

- explain the sequence of steps performed in a successful titration

- discuss the precautions necessary to ensure the accuracy of the results.

KEY WORDS

acid–base titration: a method of quantitative chemical analysis where an acid is added slowly to a base until it has been neutralised.

burette: a piece of glass apparatus used for delivering a variable volume of liquid accurately.

end point: the point in a titration where the indicator just changes colour, showing that the reaction is complete.

Focus

1   Some pieces of apparatus which may be used in a titration experiment are:

- balance
- beaker
- burette
- conical flask
- measuring cylinder
- stopwatch
- volumetric pipette.

Identify *three* pieces of apparatus which would definitely be used in a titration experiment.

State what each piece of apparatus is used for.

apparatus 1: ....

use: ....

apparatus 2: ....

use: ....

apparatus 3: ....

use: ....

2   In an acid–base titration experiment to find the concentration of ethanoic acid in a sample of vinegar, a solution of sodium hydroxide is used. Identify which other chemical is needed and state its purpose.

....

Practice

3 25 cm³ of sodium hydroxide solution was measured into a flask. Then vinegar solution was quickly run into the sodium hydroxide in the flask. The flask was swirled and the quantity of acid needed to neutralise the alkali was noted. The flask was then rinsed with distilled water. The titration was repeated more carefully a further three times. Readings from the burette are shown in Figure 12.3.

TIP

Think carefully about which solution is being added from the burette and which solution is in the flask. This will help you to understand the relationship between the volumes involved.

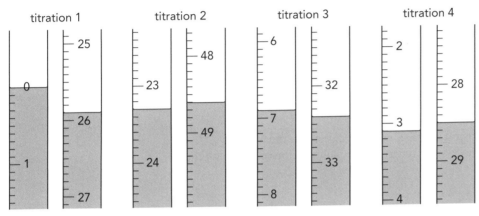

Figure 12.3: Burette readings from a titration experiment.

a Use information from Figure 12.3 to complete Table 12.5.

	Titration			
	1	**2**	**3**	**4**
Final burette reading / cm³				
First burette reading / cm³				
Volume of solution A / cm³				
Best titration result (✓)				

Table 12.5: Titration results.

b Identify which results in Table 12.5 should be disregarded. Explain your answer.

....

....

c   Calculate the mean average value obtained in the titrations.

....

d   State why the flask was swirled during the titration.

....

e   Explain why the flask was rinsed with distilled water after each titration.

....

Challenge

4 a   After rinsing, there was some distilled water remaining in the flask.
       Explain why it was not necessary to remove this water before performing the
       next titration.

....

....

....

   b   A second sample of vinegar, containing a greater concentration of ethanoic
       acid, was investigated. State whether the volumes recorded in the titration
       would be higher or lower.
       Explain your answer.

....

....

....

> Glossary

acid: a substance that dissolves in water, producing $H^+(aq)$ ions. A solution of an acid turns litmus red and has a pH below 7. Acids act as proton donors.

acid–base titration: a method of quantitative chemical analysis where an acid is added slowly to a base until it has been neutralised.

acid rain: rain that has been made more acidic than normal by the presence of dissolved pollutants such as sulfur dioxide (SO_2) and oxides of nitrogen (nitrogen oxides, NO_x).

activation energy (E_a): the minimum energy required to start a chemical reaction; for a reaction to take place, the colliding particles must possess at least this amount of energy.

addition polymer: a polymer formed by an addition reaction; the monomer molecules contain a C=C double bond.

addition reaction: a reaction in which a simple molecule adds across the carbon–carbon double bond of an alkene.

alkali: a soluble base that produces $OH^-(aq)$ ions in water – a solution of an alkali turns litmus blue and has a pH above 7.

alkali metals: elements in Group I of the Periodic Table; they are the most reactive group of metals.

alloys: mixtures of elements (usually metals) designed to have properties that are useful for a particular purpose; e.g. solder is an alloy of tin and lead, with a low melting point.

anode: the positive electrode in electrolysis.

antacids: compounds used medically to treat indigestion by neutralising excess stomach acid.

atmosphere: the layer of air and water vapour surrounding the Earth.

balanced chemical (symbol) equation: a summary of a chemical reaction using chemical formulae; the total number of any of the atoms involved is the same on both the reactant and product sides of the equation.

base: a substance that neutralises an acid, producing a salt and water as the only products. Bases act as proton acceptors.

blast furnace: a furnace for extracting metals (particularly iron) by reduction with carbon; a blast furnace uses hot air blasted in at the base of the furnace to raise the temperature.

boiling: the process of change from liquid to gas at the boiling point of the substance; a condition under which gas bubbles are able to form within a liquid – gas molecules escape from the body of the liquid, not just from its surface.

brass: an alloy of copper and zinc; this alloy is hard.

burette: a piece of glass apparatus used for delivering a variable volume of liquid accurately.

catalyst: a substance that increases the rate of a chemical reaction but itself remains unchanged at the end of the reaction.

catalytic converter: a device for converting polluting exhaust gases from cars into less dangerous emissions.

cathode: the negative electrode in electrolysis.

chemical reaction (change): a change in which a new substance is formed.

chromatogram: the result of a paper chromatography run, showing where the spots of the samples have moved to.

chromatography: a technique used to separate mixtures of dissolved substances; originally used to separate coloured dyes.

clean dry air: air containing no water vapour and only the gases which are always present in the air.

climate change: changes in weather patterns brought about by global warming.

collision theory: a theory which states that a chemical reaction takes place when particles of the reactants collide with sufficient energy to initiate the reaction.

complete combustion: a type of combustion reaction in which a fuel is burned in a plentiful supply of oxygen; the complete combustion of hydrocarbon fuels produces only carbon dioxide and water.

compound: a substance formed by the chemical combination of two or more elements in fixed proportions.

compound ion: an ion made up of several different atoms covalently bonded together and with an overall charge (can also be called a molecular ion; negatively charged compound ions containing oxygen can be called oxyanions).

concentration: a measure of how much solute is dissolved in a solvent to make a solution. Solutions can be dilute (with a high proportion of the solvent) or concentrated (with a high proportion of the solute).

condensation polymer: a polymer formed by a condensation reaction – e.g. nylon is produced by the condensation reaction between 1,6-diaminohexane and hexanedioic acid; this is the type of polymerisation used in biological systems to produce proteins, nucleic acids and polysaccharides.

covalent bonding: chemical bonding formed by the sharing of one or more pairs of electrons between two atoms.

crystallisation: the process of forming crystals from a saturated solution.

desulfurisation: an industrial process for removing contaminating sulfur from fossil fuels such as petrol (gasoline) or diesel.

diffusion: the process by which different fluids mix as a result of the random motions of their particles.

displacement reaction: a reaction in which a more reactive element displaces a less reactive element from a solution of its salt.

displayed formula: a representation of the structure of a compound which shows all the atoms and bonds in the molecule.

distillation: the process of boiling a liquid and then condensing the vapour produced back into a liquid; used to purify liquids and to separate liquids from solutions.

electrical conductor: a substance that conducts electricity but is not chemically changed in the process.

electrodes: the points where the electric current enters or leaves a battery or electrolytic cell.

electrolysis: the breakdown of an ionic compound by the use of electricity; the compound must be molten or in aqueous solution (dissolved in water).

electrolyte: an ionic compound that will conduct electricity when it is molten or dissolved in water; electrolytes will not conduct electricity when solid.

electrolytic cell: a cell consisting of an electrolyte and two electrodes (anode and cathode) connected to an external DC power source where positive and negative ions in the electrolyte are separated and discharged.

electron: a subatomic particle with negligible mass and a charge of −1; electrons are present in all atoms, located in shells (energy levels) outside the nucleus.

electronic configuration: a shorthand method of describing the arrangement of electrons within the electron shells (or energy levels) of an atom; also referred to as electronic structure.

electron shells (energy levels): (of electrons) the allowed energies of electrons in atoms; electrons fill these shells (or levels) starting with the one closest to the nucleus.

electroplating: a process of electrolysis in which a metal object is coated (plated) with a layer of another metal.

element: a substance which cannot be further divided into simpler substances by chemical methods; all the atoms of an element contain the same number of protons.

endothermic change: a process or chemical reaction which takes in heat from the surroundings.

end point: the point in a titration where the indicator just changes colour, showing that the reaction is complete.

evaporation: a process occurring at the surface of a liquid, involving the change of state from a liquid into a vapour at a temperature below the boiling point.

exothermic change: a process or chemical reaction in which heat energy is produced and released to the surroundings.

filtrate: the liquid that passes through the filter paper during filtration.

filtration: the process of separating a solid from a liquid, using a fine filter paper which does not allow the solid to pass through.

flame test: testing a compound by holding a sample in a flame to discover which colour, if any, is produced.

fossil fuels: fuels formed underground over geological periods of time from the remains of plants and animals; coal, oil and natural gas.

fractional distillation: a method of distillation using a fractionating column to separate liquids with different boiling points.

freezing point: the temperature at which a liquid turns into solid – it has the same value as the melting point; a pure substance has a sharp freezing point.

fuel: a substance that can be used as a source of energy, usually by burning (combustion).

fuel cell: a device for continuously converting chemical energy into electrical energy using a combustion reaction; a hydrogen fuel cell uses the reaction between hydrogen and oxygen.

functional group: the atom or group of atoms responsible for the characteristic reactions of a compound.

giant covalent structure: a substance where large numbers of atoms are held together by covalent bonds forming a strong lattice structure.

giant ionic lattice (structure): a lattice held together by the electrostatic forces of attraction between positive and negative ions.

global warming: a long-term increase in the average temperature of the Earth's surface, which may be caused by human activities.

greenhouse effect: the natural phenomenon in which thermal energy from the Sun is 'trapped' at the Earth's surface by certain gases in the atmosphere (greenhouse gases).

greenhouse gas: a gas that absorbs heat reflected from the surface of the Earth, stopping it escaping the atmosphere.

groups: vertical columns of the Periodic Table containing elements with similar chemical properties; atoms of elements in the same group have the same number of electrons in their outer energy levels.

half-equations: ionic equations showing the reactions at the anode (oxidation) and cathode (reduction) in an electrolytic cell.

halogen displacement reactions: reactions in which a more reactive halogen displaces a less reactive halogen from a solution of its salt.

halogens: elements in Group VII of the Periodic Table; generally the most reactive group of non-metals.

homologous series: a family of similar compounds with similar chemical properties due to the presence of the same functional group.

hydrocarbons: organic compounds that contain carbon and hydrogen only; the alkanes and alkenes are two series of hydrocarbons.

indicator: a substance which changes colour when added to acidic or alkaline solutions, e.g. litmus or thymolphthalein.

insulator: a substance that does not conduct electricity.

ionic equation: a simplified equation for a reaction involving ionic substances; only the ions which actually take part in the reaction are shown.

isotopes: atoms of the same element which have the same proton number but a different nucleon number; they have different numbers of neutrons in their nuclei; some isotopes are radioactive because their nuclei are unstable (radioisotopes).

kinetic particle theory: a theory which accounts for the bulk properties of the different states of matter in terms of the movement of particles (atoms or molecules) – the theory explains what happens during changes in physical state.

limestone: a form of calcium carbonate ($CaCO_3$).

limewater: a solution of calcium hydroxide in water; it is an alkali and is used in the test for carbon dioxide gas.

limiting reactant: the reactant that is not in excess.

litmus: the most common indicator; turns red in acid and blue in alkali.

malleable: a word used to describe a metal that can be bent and beaten into sheets.

mass concentration: the measure of the concentration of a solution in terms of the mass of the solute, in grams, dissolved per cubic decimetre of solution (g/dm^3).

melting point: the temperature at which a solid turns into a liquid – it has the same value as the freezing point; a pure substance has a sharp melting point.

methyl orange: an acid–base indicator that is red in acidic solutions and yellow in alkaline solutions.

mixture: two or more substances mixed together but not chemically combined; the substances can be separated by physical means.

molar gas volume: 1 mole of any gas has the same volume under the same conditions of temperature and pressure ($24\,dm^3$ at r.t.p.).

mole: the measure of amount of substance in chemistry; 1 mole of a substance has a mass equal to its relative formula mass in grams; that amount of substance contains 6.02×10^{23} (the Avogadro constant) atoms, molecules or formula units depending on the substance considered.

molecular formula: a formula that shows the actual number of atoms of each element present in a molecule of a compound.

monomer: a small molecule, such as ethene, which can be polymerised to make a polymer.

neutron: an uncharged subatomic particle present in the nuclei of atoms; a neutron has a mass of 1 relative to a proton.

noble gases: elements in Group VIII; a group of stable, very unreactive gases.

nucleon: a particle present in the nucleus of an atom.

ore: a naturally occurring mineral from which a metal can be extracted.

oxidation: there are three definitions of oxidation:.

i   a reaction in which oxygen is added to an element or compound.

ii a reaction involving the loss of electrons from an atom, molecule or ion.

iii a reaction in which the oxidation state of an element is increased.

particulates: very tiny solid particles produced during the combustion of fuels.

period: a horizontal row of the Periodic Table.

periodic property: a property of the elements that shows a repeating pattern when plotted against proton number (Z).

petroleum (or crude oil): a fossil fuel formed underground over many millions of years by conditions of high pressure and temperature acting on the remains of dead sea creatures.

pH scale: a scale running from below 0 to 14; use to express the acidity or alkalinity of a solution; a neutral solution has a pH of 7.

physical change: a change in the physical state of a substance or the physical nature of a situation that does not involve a change in the chemical substance(s) present.

pollutants: substances, often harmful, which are added to another substance.

polyamide: a polymer where the repeating units are joined together by amide (peptide) links, e.g. nylon and proteins.

polymer: a substance consisting of very large molecules made by polymerising a large number of repeating units (monomers).

polymerisation: the chemical reaction in which molecules (monomers) join together to form a long-chain polymer.

precipitate: an insoluble salt formed during a precipitation reaction.

precipitation: the sudden formation of a solid, either when two solutions are mixed or when a gas is bubbled into a solution.

precipitation reaction: a reaction in which an insoluble salt is prepared from solutions of two suitable soluble salts.

proton: a subatomic particle with a relative atomic mass of 1 and a charge of +1, found in the nucleus of all atoms.

proton number (or atomic number) (Z): the number of protons in the nucleus of an atom.

reaction level diagram (energy pathway diagram): a diagram that shows the energy levels of the reactants and products in a chemical reaction; it shows whether a reaction is exothermic or endothermic.

reaction rate: a measure of how fast a reaction takes place.

reactivity series of metals: an order of reactivity, giving the most reactive metal first, based on results from a range of experiments involving metals reacting with oxygen, water, dilute hydrochloric acid and metal salt solutions.

redox reaction: a reaction involving both reduction and oxidation.

reduction: there are three definitions of reduction:

i a reaction in which oxygen is removed from a compound

ii a reaction involving the gain of electrons by an atom, molecule or ion

iii a reaction in which the oxidation state of an element is decreased.

relative atomic mass (A_r): the average mass of naturally occurring atoms of an element on a scale where an atom of carbon-12 has a mass of 12 exactly.

relative formula mass (M_r): the sum of all the relative atomic masses of the atoms present in a 'formula unit' of a substance.

relative molecular mass (M_r): the sum of all the relative atomic masses of the atoms present in a molecule.

residue: the solid left behind in the filter paper after filtration has taken place.

R_f value: in chromatography, the ratio of the distance travelled by the solute to the distance travelled by the solvent front.

r.t.p.: room temperature and pressure: the standard values are 25 °C (298 K) and 101.3 kPa (1 atmosphere pressure).

rusting: the corrosion of iron and steel to form rust (hydrated iron(III) oxide).

salts: ionic compounds made by the neutralisation of an acid with a base (or alkali), e.g. copper(II) sulfate and potassium nitrate.

saturated hydrocarbons: hydrocarbon molecules in which all the carbon–carbon bonds are single covalent bonds.

slag: a molten mixture of impurities, mainly calcium silicate, formed in a blast furnace.

solubility: a measure of how much of a solute dissolves in a solvent at a particular temperature.

solvent: the liquid that dissolves a solid solute to form a solution; water is the most common solvent; other liquids in organic chemistry that can act as solvents are called organic solvents.

sonorous: a word used to describe a metallic substance that rings like a bell when hit with a hammer.

stainless steel: an alloy of iron that resists corrosion; this alloy contains a significant proportion of chromium so it is resistant to rusting.

state symbols: symbols used to show the physical state of the reactants and products in a chemical reaction: they are s (solid), l (liquid), g (gas) and aq (in solution in water).

structural formula: a representation of an organic molecule showing how all the groups of atoms are arranged in the structure; for example, the structural formula of ethanol is CH_3CH_2OH.

subatomic particles: very small particles – protons, neutrons and electrons – from which all atoms are made (*Note:* the term subatomic particles is useful but you do not need to learn it).

thermal conductivity: the ability to conduct heat.

thymolphthalein: an acid–base indicator that is colourless in acidic solutions and blue in alkaline solutions.

transition metals (transition elements): elements from the central region of the Periodic Table; they are hard, strong, dense metals that form compounds that are often coloured.

universal indicator: a mixture of indicators that has different colours in solutions of different pH.

unsaturated hydrocarbons: hydrocarbons whose molecules contain at least one carbon–carbon double or triple bond.

volumetric pipette: a pipette used to measure out a volume of solution accurately.

word equation: a summary of a chemical reaction using the chemical names of the reactants and products.

Periodic Table

The Periodic Table of Elements

Group							
I	II	III	IV	V	VI	VII	VIII

Key

atomic number
atomic symbol
name
relative atomic mass

1 H hydrogen 1																	2 He helium 4
3 Li lithium 7	4 Be beryllium 9											5 B boron 11	6 C carbon 12	7 N nitrogen 14	8 O oxygen 16	9 F fluorine 19	10 Ne neon 20
11 Na sodium 23	12 Mg magnesium 24											13 Al aluminium 27	14 Si silicon 28	15 P phosphorus 31	16 S sulfur 32	17 Cl chlorine 35.5	18 Ar argon 40
19 K potassium 39	20 Ca calcium 40	21 Sc scandium 45	22 Ti titanium 48	23 V vanadium 51	24 Cr chromium 52	25 Mn manganese 55	26 Fe iron 56	27 Co cobalt 59	28 Ni nickel 59	29 Cu copper 64	30 Zn zinc 65	31 Ga gallium 70	32 Ge germanium 73	33 As arsenic 75	34 Se selenium 79	35 Br bromine 80	36 Kr krypton 84
37 Rb rubidium 85	38 Sr strontium 88	39 Y yttrium 89	40 Zr zirconium 91	41 Nb niobium 93	42 Mo molybdenum 96	43 Tc technetium –	44 Ru ruthenium 101	45 Rh rhodium 103	46 Pd palladium 106	47 Ag silver 108	48 Cd cadmium 112	49 In indium 115	50 Sn tin 119	51 Sb antimony 122	52 Te tellurium 128	53 I iodine 127	54 Xe xenon 131
55 Cs caesium 133	56 Ba barium 137	57–71 lanthanoids	72 Hf hafnium 178	73 Ta tantalum 181	74 W tungsten 184	75 Re rhenium 186	76 Os osmium 190	77 Ir iridium 192	78 Pt platinum 195	79 Au gold 197	80 Hg mercury 201	81 Tl thallium 204	82 Pb lead 207	83 Bi bismuth 209	84 Po polonium –	85 At astatine –	86 Rn radon –
87 Fr francium –	88 Ra radium –	89–103 actinoids	104 Rf rutherfordium –	105 Db dubnium –	106 Sg seaborgium –	107 Bh bohrium –	108 Hs hassium –	109 Mt meitnerium –	110 Ds darmstadtium –	111 Rg roentgenium –	112 Cn copernicium –	113 Nh nihonium –	114 Fl flerovium –	115 Mc moscovium –	116 Lv livermorium –	117 Ts tennessine –	118 Og oganesson –

lanthanoids	57 La lanthanum 139	58 Ce cerium 140	59 Pr praseodymium 141	60 Nd neodymium 144	61 Pm promethium –	62 Sm samarium 150	63 Eu europium 152	64 Gd gadolinium 157	65 Tb terbium 159	66 Dy dysprosium 163	67 Ho holmium 165	68 Er erbium 167	69 Tm thulium 169	70 Yb ytterbium 173	71 Lu lutetium 175
actinoids	89 Ac actinium –	90 Th thorium 232	91 Pa protactinium 231	92 U uranium 238	93 Np neptunium –	94 Pu plutonium –	95 Am americium –	96 Cm curium –	97 Bk berkelium –	98 Cf californium –	99 Es einsteinium –	100 Fm fermium –	101 Md mendelevium –	102 No nobelium –	103 Lr lawrencium –

The volume of one mole of any gas is 24 dm³ at room temperature and pressure (r.t.p.).

> Acknowledgements

The authors and publishers acknowledge the following sources of copyright material and are grateful for the permissions granted. While every effort has been made, it has not always been possible to identify the sources of all the material used, or to trace all copyright holders. If any omissions are brought to our notice, we will be happy to include the appropriate acknowledgements on reprinting.

Thanks to the following for permission to reproduce images:

Cover: Sebastien GABORIT/Getty Images; *Inside:* Figure 1.6 ANDREW LAMBERT PHOTOGRAPHY / SCIENCE PHOTO LIBRARY; Figure 9.5 ZHMURCHAK/Shutterstock